First Sight

First Sight

The Experience of Faith

Laurence Freeman

continuum

Published by the Continuum International Publishing Group

The Tower Building	80 Maiden Lane
11 York Road	Suite 704
London SE1 7NX	New York NY 10038

www.continuumbooks.com

First published 2011

British Library Cataloguing-in-Publication Data
A catalogue record for this book is available from the British Library.

ISBN: 978-1-4411-6157-4

Typeset by Newgen Imaging Systems Pvt Ltd, Chennai, India
Printed and bound in Great Britain

For
Anne, Jack, Sean, Kieran, Aidan, Liam and Aisling

May you have the faith which depends on you and is directed to God, so that you may receive from God also that faith which transcends human capacity.

St Cyril of Jerusalem

We need to be faithful. We have to learn to be faithful.

John Main

Fellowship arises because we all live by faith in spite of the diversity of our beliefs.

Ramon Pannikar

Contents

Introduction   ix

1. Understanding Faith   1

2. Process and Lifestyle   16

3. The Power of Faith   31

4. Stages of Faith: Purgation   43

5. Stages of Faith: Illumination   59

6. Stages of Faith: Union   72

7. Christian Faith   96

8. Unity   120

Afterword   132
Starting to Meditate   134
Suggested Reading   147

Introduction

When does a journey of faith begin? In the womb as, pre-conceptually, we first experience relationship? Or even, as St Augustine and others of the early Christian thinkers speculated, before conception? In any case, it is through the imperfect function of memory that the first stages of our journey of faith takes shape in the mists of the unknown sources of the self.

I was sitting in a classroom with my classmates waiting for the first religion class of the new term. We had successfully sent the previous religion teacher packing with, what we hoped with the cruelty of our age, was a nervous breakdown. He had showed his weakness to us and we remorselessly exploited it and ran riot. Flushed with this success we anticipated the new teacher of this soft subject as a similar victim. We were encouraged in this by knowing that he was 'only a brother', Brother John, not yet a priest. Of course, priests were not exempt from our battle to dominate the classroom but you had to be more careful with them.

When Brother John entered the room all eyes were on him, seeking to get the measure of the man in those vital few moments that largely determine the future of relationships in life. He was smiling and that surprised us as he showed none of the fear or nervousness we expected of a new teacher. It was as if he knew us already and, with all our faults, understood and accepted us. Br John was tall, always a help in leadership roles, and he seemed from the first moment to be competent and ready to take control. As the class began we saw and admired his manner which was friendly but detached. Later he told me the secret of school teaching was to treat the children as adults, as far as they were able to accept it, but never to forget they were children. Many years later meeting with old friends from the same class we recalled this moment and surprisingly many recalled the story he told about Mrs Jones and her new fridge. This, I think, was intended to illustrate the meaning of idolatry. His style of teaching meant that his stories stayed in the minds of his students for decades.

Over the next few years I got to know Dom John, now ordained, as we called him. We saw him as more sophisticated than the other monks and though he enforced the rules, petty as some seemed, did so with irony. We knew he disapproved of corporal punishment which put him on the revolutionary side. At meals in the refectory I would often sit next to him and he allowed us to argue with him about politics and religion. Our little group of boys were surprised, some shocked, that he saw nothing wrong in an atheistic head of government.

At the end of my last term I told him I was going to be in the United States for a year. He invited me to visit him in Washington where he was going to become headmaster of Benedictine School. Years later I realized what a time of personal suffering this move was for him. He showed none of it when he said I would be welcome to visit. For my part I was just happy to have a friendly contact in a new land. But I forgot to get his address. Rushed along on the wave of my newfound freedom I would probably never have troubled to contact him and get it. But as I was leaving the school building for the last time I met him by chance in the doorway as he was coming in. He wished me well and I remembered then to get his address, scribbling it on a scrap of paper that I kept safe with my new passport when I got home.

I have often wondered since then how much small, random incidents shape the big pictures of our lives.

INTRODUCTION

My generation grew into consciousness in the aftermath of the worst nightmares of the twentieth century. As a young boy, born in the year wartime rationing ended, I remember seeing the bombsites in London waiting for the development boom, hearing stories of the Blitz from its survivors it and sensing even then how those traumatic times were for many the most alive times of their lives. I also tasted for a while, before the economic resurgence, what austerity really meant: the low-cost, non-disposable pleasures that preceded our era of extravagance, pollution and waste. The Holocaust, too, was beginning to find its narrators and as their stories penetrated our cultural self-confidence, through book, film and academic papers, these fresh memories shook our faith in the conventions of civilization. Our parents' generation had generated barbarism. With America's might the world set about putting this past behind it. However, there was hardly time to recover from the nightmare of two world wars before the shadow of the cold war fell over us with its paranoia and the insanities and inanity of the arms race.

The Sixties came as a huge relief, a shaking off of the past and a new idealism and unbounded confidence in the future. Our generation were not responsible for the horrors the previous one had perpetrated on their watch. We were free from them, free from history, free to explore and enjoy the world and its marvels. Looking back all seemed doom and gloom, with a few streaks of glory and heroism captured by Hollywood. But looking ahead there was science and technology that would free us from myth and solve our problems and answer our questions. Above all, there was affluence and, especially for adolescents in the Sixties, a new, intoxicating sexual freedom. Studying literature I could feel that the early Romantics were our contemporaries and the future was a new and inviting country:

Bliss was it in that dawn to be alive,
But to be young was very heaven! – Oh! times,

INTRODUCTION

In which the meagre, stale, forbidding ways
Of custom, law, and statute, took at once
The attraction of a country in romance!
(Wordsworth, *The French Revolution as it Appeared to its Enthusiasts at it Commencement*)

We were the new Romantics, even more daring. As with Wordsworth, my generation has since felt betrayed by these hopes for a new social order. Our euphoria of freedom from the tentacles of past led us somehow into new forms of restraint. Predictably the next generation blindly obeys the law of the pendulum. Many young people today tend, to the degree that they feel involved in political questions at all, towards security and conservatism rather than idealism. A new sense of powerlessness has crept up on us. The forces of globalization, the hidden levers of power behind the show of democracy make us feel little we can do makes a difference. The deconstruction of social welfare accompanies a retreat into privatization of the self. In the lobby of a concert hall recently I watched a group of people gyrating to music that they heard through individual headphones that each was wearing.

This lost conservatism and disconnected individualism is often reflected, too, in religious taste. One of my American students surprised me by his attraction to, if not infatuation with, Tridentine ritual and paraphernalia. He loved all the restored details of the old liturgy, putting on the surplice and serving Benediction, swinging the thurible and learning Latin hymns. These were religious pleasures of my own boyhood but I could not help feeling they had a different meaning for him. For me they were what was there already. For him, it was consciously a restored fashion. The priest who celebrated this kind of liturgy welcomed the involvement of this kind of intelligent and good-natured young man; then to his surprise and disappointment the priest discovered the student had missed out on the first step of becoming a Catholic and did not seem to think that it was particularly necessary. For the priest this was serious error. The Catholic Mass and rules of the church had been disrespected. For the student, reared on choice and diversity, this was one among many ways of exploring his religious feelings. Postmodern traditionalism often isn't what it seems to those who grew up with it and pray for its restoration.

I have written a book about faith with this kind of young seeker (rather than the priest with the backward glance) in mind – a young person, often rootless, but looking for roots from which to grow, a product of fashion yet sensing that what they are looking for may be found in the treasure chests of tradition which have been relegated to the attics or basements of the social construct that formed them. I have also written this book on faith, with faith in them. The young meditators in our meditation community have taught me much of what is in the following pages. They have given me hope and expectation to balance my disillusionment with recent history. Although it may not reach many of their age group, it may be of interest to others who work with them and who are concerned for the generation who are now inheriting the material with which they will write the next chapter of the book of humanity.

After the cold war came the absolute triumph of one of the two competing ideologies. It soon became evident that neither capitalism nor communism had really had sincere proponents. All kinds of idealism were tainted and the ancient virtues seemed quaint in a world where 'greed is good' and wealth could be conjured out of computers. The word 'freedom' was found to have been hollowed out. It meant my doing what I wanted. Once the capitalist West won the war a consumer surge drowned the language of idealism which mutated into a vocabulary justifying refined forms of exploitation and injustice such as the 'rising tide' theory. The more wealth that was created would trickle down and all would rise happily together. Yet, as the tide rose it became clear how many people were being left behind in the sludge. The chasm between the rich and the poor – as old as any monetary economy – took on new proportions of inequality. Social discourse – that is, most of the news items that were not about sex crimes or celebrities – was dominated by the 'economy' just as political comment focused on personality and effectiveness of journalistic spin rather than content. This environment – individualism, consumerism and the sound byte – quickly (everything happened quickly) became the matrix of a new subjective morality and a diminishing sense of virtue and meaning. In fact, it presaged a shrinking of the collective soul into to a fantastic hyper-individualism as Margaret Thatcher infamously illustrated by her belief that 'there is no such thing as society'. As with Marie Antoinette's advice to the breadless poor to eat cake, this dramatized an extreme point of social aberration.

Before long the dams holding back the tide of reality broke and the age of greed foundered on its own success. In the reconstruction process a new world is being born. Cultural and economic centres of gravity are shifting. The future is unclear but we have a chance again to do better. When crisis hits, no one welcomes it because it involves a frightening and disorienting loss of control. But from the deep fissures opened up by the earthquake new ways of seeing, a resurgence of wisdom, can emerge.

The first monks of the Christian tradition, the 'desert fathers and mothers' of the fourth and fifth centuries, fled the world of a collapsing empire. They left the crowd to seek God and to learn to pray in a radical lifestyle of simplicity, solitude and community. Their psychological insight into the human quest for wholeness – simply 'seeking God', as St Benedict calls it – led them to categorize certain states of mind which they aptly called demons. These 'eight principal faults' were later domesticated as the 'seven deadly sins'. In our predicament this early but archetypal system of Christian self-knowledge and self-correction is particularly useful because, it has the kind of

INTRODUCTION

pragmatic rationalism that has made Buddhism so attractive. The desert teachers did not split hairs. They didn't count how many angels could dance on the head of a pin. They did not try to restore an old liturgy. Rather than inducing guilt and discouragement, their morality was therapeutic and proposed remedies.

The distinction they make, for example, between Gluttony and Greed helps us to see ourselves more clearly in a culture of, on the one hand, obesity, addiction and excess and, on the other, universal debt and over the top bankers' bonuses. In an age where pornography is a global industry Fornication has important meaning. As ever, Envy can determine political policies as much as facts and statistics. Anger is rampant with new intensities – from videogames, binge drinking and child abuse to international terrorism against commuters or foreign aid workers. In a society where depression has become endemic Sadness seeks a cure – increasingly in meditation as well as medication. *Acedia*, dropped in the later accounts of the desert wisdom, is no less with us – a gnawing hunger for the unattainable and discontent with what we have. Vainglory is the demon of celebrity, and Pride, the Achilles' heel of a culture of narcissism.

Our time is not so different from past times when we see it in this way, but it dramatizes on a quite new scale the script that human beings have worked on since the beginning. We therefore have much greater potential for harm and damage to our future. In the attempt to be fully human and find happiness we frequently trade our inheritance for a 'mess of pottage' – as Esau gave up his birthright for a bowl of lentil stew. Again there is nothing new in this except perhaps – and this is dangerous in a new way – the weakening awareness of what happiness and fulfilment means, what we are capable of and the loss of a common language about what we are losing. Identity is an intense concern of our time. It drives innumerable ethnic,

CuriousLlama

local wars. The sense of losing personal identity and the meaning that it gives to life, undermines the mental health of an increasing proportion of Western society. As we approach the new age of bio-engineering it has never been more crucial that we retain the most obvious of all qualities of the human – a feel for what human means.

All of this recent history and the anxiety and confusion we feel about the future lead us to the question of faith.

It is why I feel that exploring the meaning of this little monosyllable can help refocus us. It can clarify our crisis and reveal not only its dangers but its opportunities. Understanding faith re-connects a culture of frenetic immediacy to the peace of the present moment through the forgotten life-giving resources of our heritage. Faith, I would like to say, is about a way of seeing and consequently about a way of living. I certainly have not exhausted its meaning in the following pages. But maybe it offers food for thought that will lead to the even more transformational work of what the desert teachers called meditation – pure prayer or the 'laying aside of thoughts'.

Faith, as I understand it, means an unpredictable journey rather than a value of fixed content. It is an inborn capacity of humanity that makes growth and development happen. As we grow, so does faith, and we grow the more by exercising this capacity. More, not less, faith is needed for the different but often interconnecting journeys of education, marriage, friendship, social participation and the interior journey of meditation. All these are aspects of our human development between birth and death through many micro-cycles of death and rebirth towards the final liberation from the cycle, the great resurrection. All these aspects both need and deepen faith. Faith is mysterious because it is renewable energy of expansion on a self-transcending scale that runs from the personal to the cosmic.

But when does any journey really begin? As with map-making we look at things differently according to what it is we are specifically looking for. If we are looking for a gas station we are not so interested in ancient monuments. But on a life-journey the stages we pass through acquire canonical status in our lives. To other eyes they may seem unremarkable events. For us, personally, they come to be seen as major milestones whose meanings we will not cease to fathom and that we will relive, if we have the time, at the moment of death. They connect up in memory and imagination and form a pattern that we make into a story. (For me meditation is such a pattern.) They make stories that often impart more meaning than commentaries. So I offer a little relief from these chapters about seeking the meaning of faith by recalling some of my own milestones on the way of meditation which is pre-eminently a way of faith.

Laurence Freeman OSB
Bere Island, October 2010

1

Understanding Faith

During the first hectic week at university I was occasionally noticing messages from my brother in Australia. Then one came urgently from the chaplaincy saying he was trying to find me. I realized that it wasn't just wishing me good luck. In those pre-mobile phone days we had to go to a telephone box located in the old narrow, barrel-vaulted passage that led from the new to the medieval quadrangle. It was a dark, rainy autumnal night. I couldn't get an answer from home so finally called a cousin whose deep intake of breath when she heard my voice made me realize I was in for bad news. When she told me, my knees collapsed – it has never happened to me since – and I crumpled to the ground.

After my sister's funeral I returned to Oxford and tried to catch up with my studies. It was good to have that challenge but beneath the rush of activity there ran a river of deep grief and perhaps an even deeper flood of meaninglessness. I must have written to Fr John in Washington about these confused and often overwhelming emotions because after a few months he asked me if I would like to go and spend Easter in the monastery. Later I realized he was a little concerned about my balance of mind.

He and the other monks in Washington were very kind. I had never noticed the humane side of monastic life before and this, I suppose, was to have an effect on me; but it was the conversations I had with Fr John in his office in the school that mattered most. He made time for me despite his busy schedule. He had just been appointed headmaster and was dealing with a multiple crisis but I never realized this, as he was always completely centred, attentive and present. We must have talked about everything from my immediate feelings to the big questions of God and Life but I cannot remember these talks.

What I remember is a conversation which ended with him introducing me to meditation. In a very few words, lightly delivered, he sprinkled this teaching on my troubled mind. He didn't give the impression that he was saying that I should meditate or even that it would be good for me. I was just told how to do it. Although I had been reading very eclectically in mystical literature and must have come across meditation very often, this was a completely new revelation to me. I had no idea at all what it meant. My intellectual search had prepared me very little, it seemed, for the practice.

I was intrigued but could not understand why. I tried to meditate and had about as much success as I did when my elder brother pushed me in at the deep end of the pool to teach me how to swim. Several times I suggested to Fr John we meditate together but I don't recall doing so at that time. He left the seed to grow in its own time. And slowly it did. When I returned to Oxford I felt better able to cope and did a bit of meditation when I was feeling low or had nothing better to do.

I would meet with Fr John when he returned to London during vacation times. I discovered a strong affinity in humour and interests and learned much just by being with him. Once after, in good English Benedictine style, we had had lunch at his club in Pall Mall we stood outside on the pavement saying goodbye. Shaking hands, a silent exchange or transmission took place between us. I suppose an Indian or indeed a contemporary disciple of Jesus might have called it initiation by a glance. It was silent, impossible to analyse yet it revealed, in a new moment and new way, something that had always been.

UNDERSTANDING FAITH

Many of us today feel that we are inhabiting a 'secular age'. In a long and complex process this has succeeded an 'age of faith'. What an age of faith means is itself problematical – probably it means a religious society and culture in which there was general consensus about beliefs and morality. That, the story goes, was eroded by the unstoppable forces of modernity – hard-won social freedoms, a new sense of selfhood, techno-science, education, encounters with other cultures, all draining away the spiritual authority of institutional religion. But is this understanding of our modern culture wholly accurate or helpful? For many people the answer is personally important for their peace of mind and style of life – the values by which we live. It is not just interesting for social philosophers and theologians. However much the great ship of religion may be sinking, we remain spiritual in our needs and aspirations. If we see that religion has a fleet rather than a single battleship, we can see how certain types of old time religion are being taken out of service but other religious forms of are under construction. This generation spans the transition. Although we suffer the insecurity of such times we also enjoy the excitement of seeing the new take shape and also the responsibility for contributing to the direction in which we are moving.

We still seek wholeness. It is intrinsic to human identity that, however much we have achieved, we are never satisfied. We hunger and thirst for what lies beyond our grasp and even beyond the horizon of our desire. Religion and spirituality, which are less easy to divorce than we thought – are the elements of culture that deal with this desire beyond desire. Where are they taking us? Where do we have to redefine the old terms by which we try to understand ourselves in this longing for wholeness?

Does secular, for example, always mean faith-less?

*

The melancholy and self-inflicted wounds of conventional religion and the dramatic, scary rise of fundamentalist religion

3

catch the headlines; but there is also another and, I will suggest here, a more significant kind of religion taking shape around us. This is the resurgence on an unprecedented scale of the contemplative dimension – indeed the heart – of religion. It has always been there, usually marginalized, sometimes persecuted and has regularly surged in certain periods to challenge the sclerosis and cleanse the arteries of religion. The Sufis of Islam or the mystics of Christianity speak to their spiritual descendants today as if they are our contemporaries. Indeed, in a sense they are. Although we have to adjust to their historically conditioned language and thought, the essence of what they have left us has not passed its use-by date. This is not surprising as what they are concerned with and communicate to us is the timeless.

> The inner Light is beyond praise and blame; like space, it knows no boundaries, yet it is even here, within us, ever retaining its serenity and fullness. It is only when you hunt for it that you lose it. You cannot take hold of it, but equally, you cannot get rid of it. (Yung-Chia-Ta-Shih, 7th century)
>
> Christ Jesus is the same yesterday, today and tomorrow. (Heb. 13:8)

Today, as traditional forms of institutional religion mutate – this change cannot be measured only by attendance at places of worship – spirituality expands exponentially. This indicates an intensified quest for a form of religious consciousness that arises from and relates to personal concerns and our day-to-day lives. We yearn for a religious experience arising from the indwelling truth of our most real selves. Yet we know intuitively that this inner experience must be connected to and be of benefit to others and to all aspects of our own humanity. If the experience remains self-fixated it degenerates. In the same way eros that does not, at the right moment expand into agape, slowly dies or becomes violent. The 'spiritual' that is not moving into other-centredness and a more inclusive love is just fashion. Through the rise of authentic spirituality, new forms of a less dogmatic, rigid and ritualistic religion are forming. Along with interior experience, self-awareness and transformation we yearn for connection with others even as we enter upon this most solitary of levels. A spirituality that does not form some kind of community remains superficial.

This generation – comprising people of all ages – seeks God regardless of our scepticism about clerical hierarchies, God's professional representatives on earth. Today people look for teachers not preachers. Strongly secular countries like Australia show a deep attraction to meditation and form strong communities from the shared practice of silence and stillness. Elsewhere, still strongly religious societies, such as in South America, are passing through religious change though perhaps less radically than in Europe. Many Latin Americans and Asians remain loyal to their traditional forms of religion, especially the 'new Christians'; but in large numbers they too seek the lost contemplative dimension of their faith and wonder how to integrate it with the social gospel of justice and solidarity with the poor. The marriage of contemplation and action which is at the heart of any living faith is manifesting in many new forms of religion today.

Taking a global view of religion, then, it is naive to say that faith is evaporating even in materialistic, secular societies. The experience of the southern hemisphere and of Asia, not less than the religious developments in Africa, can help Westerners understand better what is happening to their traditions of faith. Financially the centre of power has already migrated from west to east although many Westerners still think of the world economy as centred on themselves. Spiritually too, it may be time for the West to look to the East, not as an alternative to their traditional faith but as a way of renewing and reappropriating it. In this exploration of the meaning of faith today I am focusing on the Western experience, but aware that faith is a universal and unifying human phenomenon. In some form or other faith is present – or present by its absence – in all human experience. What happens to the practice of faith in one part of the family eventually affects us all. Recovering a better sense of what faith means will help us in negotiating the global crisis of the human family and planetary home. This is why faith is important to understand.

I will try to make this a practice-oriented exploration. What can we do – spiritually speaking – to understand faith today and to put that understanding at the service of the needs of our time? The practice I will concentrate on is meditation. John Main says that meditation is a 'way of faith', the quintessential prayer of faith. Meditation develops the practical orientation of faith in all areas of life. It is universal, found in all religious traditions. And it is simple. Because we can so easily teach children to meditate it is a realistic way of giving global change a new direction by developing the consciousness of the next generation.

John Main says that meditation is a way of faith because he saw that in meditation

> We have to leave ourselves behind before the other appears and without the pre-packaged guarantee that the other will appear. (John Main, *Word into Silence*, p. 21)

This is a good way of beginning our exploration of faith – by facing the uncertainty principle. You never know anything for sure. This might suggest that faith is a kind of gamble. Whenever we make a gesture or 'act' of faith, we take a calculated risk; we don't know how it will turn out or whether it will backfire. Who knows whether we are going to get anything back on our investment because we can never predict the future with certainty? Modern physics tells us that at the deeper levels of the observable material world we find the same situation as in the human realm. Probability rules. The only certainty is that nothing is certain. But there is actually one thing we can be totally certain about. At some moment in the future we will take our last breath. Death is the only predictable certainty. So probability is not unique to an act of faith. When we commit ourselves to someone or something into the future or transcend ourselves we are taking a risk and stepping into the unknown; but that's simply *life*. Everything is uncertain. The deeper insight into faith that John Main is giving us involves the conscious and voluntary *laying down* of our life, the conscious act of leaving self behind. Transcendence, then, not certainty of belief, is the essence of faith.

*

Christianity today has embarked on a radicalizing project: of recovering and updating the contemplative dimension in all aspects of its life – dialogue with the secular and scientific worlds and with other religions, and also, at home, in its theology, morality, prayer, worship and social action. If the church fails in this spiritualizing endeavour or yields to the temptation to regress into a nostalgic world of supposed certainties, as some would like, it will be impossible for it to adjust to a secular world and be what it is meant to be. Today Christian identity itself – the reception and communication of what comes to humanity through Jesus – is at stake. A corollary of this identity is its relationship to other religious identities and its need to be a team-player with other forms of faith in responding to the global crisis.

Unless it is contemplative, the church fails to be contemporary. Its 'catholicity' – that is, its universality – contracts. As it contracts to near-extinction it shrivels into being a mere cult. It is not, however, the size of its congregations that matters but the quality of mind awakened in those who go to church or don't go to church conventionally at all but live the Christian faith in other ways. Numbers go up and down. Mind is trans-numerical. It is either open or closed or it tends in one of these directions. The world needs contemplatives with courageously open minds of whatever form of faith– Buddhists, Hindus, Jews or Muslims. Every religion faces its particular challenge to recover and reconnect with its spiritual core. Christianity needs contemplative Christians, coming from their experience of this centre and carrying the Word of a unifying gospel into a wounded world bent on self-destruction. Mission is an element of Christian discipleship – to go forth and speak of the experience of faith. Where faith is strong, conversion is not the goal of mission. That is the work of the Spirit not a human project. So the mission of the contemporary Christian is essentially contemplative and will lead into dialogue rather than sheep-stealing. Contemplatives are made from experience that runs on pure faith. This is why we need to understand what faith means. This may require many Christians to undergo a deprogramming of their earlier religious training. They must first allow themselves to be converted.

This prayer is a typical 'act of faith' that many once learned by heart when they were young. It is and was meant to be formative, clear and reassuring. It suggests an enticing certainty that truth can be caught in a verbal formula. But it can also testify to a moving and simple humility, daring to try to put the mystery into which faith leads us into words. Simple childlike clarity of this kind can however easily be hijacked and lead to a closed mind where humility mutates into hubris.

Oh my God I firmly believe that thou art one God in three divine persons, Father, Son and Holy Spirit. I believe that this divine Son became man and died for our sins, and that he will come to judge the living and the dead. I believe these and all the truths which the holy Catholic Church teaches because thou hast revealed them, who can neither deceive nor be deceived.

Such an 'act of faith' is not inauthentic. There is something simple and mysterious about it. The crafted phrases are, however, pointers to faith rather than an expression of it. It is not essentially an act of faith at all but a statement of belief. It expresses faith in one dimension which is personal or collective belief – *I believe*. Christians have often limited their understanding of faith to what they believe or, even worse, to what they feel they have to believe in order 'to be saved'. If only we were saved – brought to the fullness of our humanity – by what we believe it would be much easier, but far less human. Human flourishing happens not through what we say but through what we do and learn, what we *become* through repeated and sustained acts of faith. When belief takes the place of faith in the religious mind the possible range of spiritual experience and growth is critically limited. When religion emphasizes belief rather than faith it may find it easier to organize and define its membership and those it excludes. It is easier to pass judgement. But it will produce, at the best, half-formed followers. The road to transcendence is cut off, blocked by landfalls of beliefs as immoveable as boulders, beliefs we are told to accept and do not dare to put to the test of experience. In such a rigid and enforced belief-system what I believe also easily slides into what I *say* I believe, or what I am told to believe or what I feel I ought to believe, because the *I* that believes becomes so dependent on the identity generated by the structured belief system we inhabit.

*

Instead of fingers pointing to the moon, doctrine or dogma bend backwards pointing to themselves. Anything that questions belief is then perceived as threatening and what is threatening can exude a kind of strangeness or threat which incites fear. *I am what I believe* is as dangerous a principle as *I am because I think*. What I want or try to believe then constitutes my identity, my self, and so because I believe in these doctrines I am a

Christian. Others who don't believe these particular statements are 'non-believers'. Belief may indeed be strong and true. We can be loyal to our beliefs and die to defend the system they form part of. But belief of this kind – the kind we might die for – should arise from the experience of faith not the fear of a threatened and insecure identity. Why die or attack others over verbal formulas alone? As long as we think of faith as constituted by belief, we lack the full dimension of the mind of Christ. This means the 'catholic' mind that inherently seeks to include and integrate rather than to exclude and condemn when it meets with different expressions of belief that bring the natural uncertainty in our own system to the surface. We see that there are different ways of belief and that others may hold theirs as sincerely as we hold ours. Without faith we will feel painfully threatened by this. Reacting from our insecurity, Christians often describe devout followers of other religious traditions as 'non-believers' simply because they have different beliefs.

Differences, like opposites, are only ultimately resolved in God who is infinitely simple enough to contain it all. Only in God can we meet others and it is at the level of faith, not belief, that this meeting occurs. Monks from different religions meet and instantly recognize something in common with each other, deep and subtle, despite the differences between them. So, in another way, do football supporters from different teams (sometimes) or people new to parenthood. Whoever has faith recognizes it in another and feels connected to them through it, however widely their different beliefs may separate them.

In a time like ours that values – at least notionally – tolerance of differences, the new arts of inter-religious dialogue have taught many how to accept that we live by different beliefs from other people but that differences need not become divisions. I am not saying beliefs are unimportant. Differences are as important as similarities in any human encounter. Beliefs have not just intellectual significance. They combine with culture to shape the ways we make meaning and the ways we live that meaning. The Buddhist or Hindu who believes in reincarnation and the Christian who believes, not in rebirth but in a realm of purification in the next life, hold not only different symbolic ideas about the meaning and nature of a human life but they live out these beliefs in cultures shaped by them. Attitudes to social or personal transformation may be shaped by these beliefs; they may generate tolerance or passivity, anxiety or passion for justice as recognizable psycho-cultural characteristics. Yet also, between different beliefs deep resonances can be detected despite the impossibility of ever achieving an exact translation between them. For these reasons, there is always the possibility of conversation and therefore mutual enrichment between different beliefs, even or especially when they appear to contradict one another. As we meet and connect with those who believe differently from ourselves we discover in the realm of difference itself the mystery of a common ground. Within the rich diversity of humanity there is a unity that all, even the non-human, share. Monotheistic religions, believe in the oneness of God who creates and delights in diversity. The unity is in the inherent image God that every kind of being contains as its true nature and expresses by virtue of its own unique manifestation of selfhood. This corresponds to the intrinsic emptiness of all beings in Buddhist thought as it does to the atman–Brahman equivalence in Hindu thought. Not the same, but deeply similar. The Buddhist belief in Buddha nature, the Hindu belief in atman and Brahman resonate – they do not translate – with the Logos philosophy of the biblical tradition. Truth waits to be discovered in this resonance not in a quest for uniformity of belief.

Faith, as we shall see, is the frequency of that resonance. The gift of the monotheistic tradition is its perception of the unity of the human resonating with the oneness of God. 'May they all be one', Jesus prayed. His followers don't, it is true, hold a great record of putting this belief into practice – or of being faithful to it – but they have had their good moments. Unity in diversity is an essential principle in our tradition and it cannot be disowned without eroding Christian identity. That identity is important not only to those who hold it but also to those who bear a different identity. China's investments in the United States are devaluing steadily but it is more in her interest to keep them there because it needs the United States as a market for its goods. Globalization at an economic level thinly reflects the deeper inter-dependence of religions and culture in the human family. Everybody needs others to be themselves. This is our fundamental unity.

The oneness of things is not reducible to a belief. We look at beliefs directly and analyse them. This is an intuition, a sapiential insight arising from contemplative experience. We see it more clearly with peripheral vision, more by *unknowing* than by dissection. Recovering the contemplative dimension of Christian life has therefore made it more possible to embark upon both inter-religious dialogue and the cooperation of religions in the field of global action. The believer who rejects this form of contemplative knowing remains imprisoned in belief systems; and the doctrines he holds become the bars that separate him from others. For such a prisoner of belief even to be in dialogue with others seems like a betrayal of his belief.

A new understanding of faith demolishes the prison of belief. It liberates religious people into a world of compassionate action expressed in the parable of the Good Samaritan. No one is excluded from this extension of the experience of unity arising from the depths of the soul into which beliefs cannot penetrate because 'we know God not by thought but by love'. In the horizons revealed by the light of contemplative experience we no longer identify faith with belief or condemn other people's beliefs as deficient. The contemplative should have a more Christ-like courtesy than that. And in the risk – yes there is a risk involved – of encountering the other, meeting other believers in the strange realms of difference, we discover the

nature of faith itself. We are also reassured that our own identity that we feared was threatened is in fact affirmed.

*

To go back to the 'act of faith' I quoted above, it's not that the
Christian doesn't believe these statements about ultimate reality, the nature of God, the relationship of Jesus to the Father in
the Holy Spirit, and so on. But in the contemplative 'catholic'
mind that is awakened by the unknowing and the peripheral
vision of meditation the new energy of faith is generated. It is
not limited to belief in statements (however true and wonderful) though it may pervade them and make them more richly
symbolic and evocative. Faith is always more than an assertion
of belief, however vigorous, sincere or beautifully expressed
that assertion may be. Faith is also more than a special identity
that we hold and defend, making us different from (and often
implicitly superior to) other people only because we believe
different things. Faith is not just the resolve to stick to our
beliefs by saying

> I'm holding on to these beliefs however irrational they
> may seem, however much the world may mock me for
> holding these beliefs, however my culture, my society or
> intellectual opposition may challenge these beliefs. I'm
> going to hang on to them and defend these beliefs.

Faith will make us question what we most deeply believe and
help us see why they should be held to.

Merely asserting and defending our beliefs cannot lead to a
true community of faith. They make us become sect-members,
a fundamentalist cabal. They shut down the mind as an organ
of perception and truth. If, by confusing faith and belief in
this way, we think of faith as bestowing a sense of being different or superior to others we end up like the Pharisee who
thanked God for making him different from others and found

satisfaction in being superiorly different. The religious mind in this state can even persuade itself that this is humility. Identifying entirely with belief – the left hand hemisphere of the brain – while denying faith – the right-hand hemisphere – we occupy a private world of our own rather than the kingdom of God or the Christ-realm in which 'there is neither Jew nor Greek, male of female, slave nor free'. Religious people often fear the power of faith precisely because it tends towards this undifferentiated realm of the Spirit where religious, social and even gender differences that our enshrined beliefs can control minutely, are all dismantled.

Faith is the highway to the spirit. Every act of faith we make is an uncovering of the labyrinth of spirit. Belief, sundered from faith, leads to a maze of mirrors, a series of infinite regressions, the egotistical maze. Mazes lead to dead-ends and the more we get lost the more we panic. Labyrinths only ask us to follow faithfully their strange but ultimately symmetrical loops and bends in order to lead us home to the centre.

Confusing faith with belief and so separating them traps us in the Law – within things we can define, regulations we can enforce, specific creedal formulas that justify us in rejecting others. More than any other religion Christianity has fallen into the temptations of power that uniformity of belief creates. Worshipping orthodoxy of belief – getting the words, rituals, externals and formulas exactly right – betrays the living God for a false one of our own construction. Difference has to be understood in the light of faith even within religious traditions. All religions have their internal differences calling intra-religious dialogue. The Jews say if you have three rabbis discussing a point of the law you will end up with four different opinions. Sunnis and Shiites, Mahayana and Theravada Buddhists, Catholics and Protestants all hold different beliefs within the same faith-tradition. Some may even feel or be closer to believers in other religions than they are with their fellow believers. We can draw a flow chart of the relationships between religions that accentuate this inter-connectivity more than the distances between them. But Christianity, perhaps more than any other tradition, has tried to impose uniformity most harshly at times and has therefore acted contrary to the mind of Christ by falling into the trap of exclusion and excommunication. The days of the Inquisition or the wars of religion are over, but the embarrassing, shameful divisions within the Christian world and the levels of anger they generate against each other testify to that same failure of faith even today.

Belief can be heroic. You can refuse to disown your beliefs and may be happy to be burned at the stake or stripped of rank and status for them. Many believers are raised with stories of these heroic martyrs, who laid down their lives rather than disown their beliefs. We shouldn't diminish the heroism of belief in the face of oppression and persecution. Strength and integrity are required to resist the violent force that would make us disown our principles and beliefs. But the spiritual realm is not about heroism. The heroic mentality of the warrior – or martyr – yields to another kind of self-awareness once we experience God as love, rather than the bestower of fame or eternal glory. Achilles is admirable, but he is not a saint. Thomas More is a hero of religious freedom and personal integrity rather than a teacher of the mysteries. Faith is more than the most heroic belief. It is not only a passionately held conviction, however loyal and self-sacrificing the conviction. Faith is more than a concept and more than a sign of loyal belonging to a particular group.

It is relationship with what we believe; with what we believe because we experience it and with what we experience because we are simply designed for it. And by it. Faith plunges us into ontology and endlessly reveals the full extent of the mysteries of being.

2

Process and Lifestyle

I began to see that I had decided against an academic career. It was too predictable for me and I was eager for adventure, escape and experience on a richer scale. I started by teaching which is a good way to de-condition oneself after 10 years on the education conveyor belt. In the light of my interests and lack of numeracy banking represented a completely unlikely option. I was not so much interested in making money as I was curious to learn how it was made. I became a suburban commuter. Every day, at the same time, I walked to Wimbledon station, fought for a seat to Waterloo, and was swept along in the Drain, the underground link to the City. It was immersion in the mass but curiously reassuring. Unpredictability was limited to late trains – and that was a frequent occasion for collective complaint. I sensed how easily any routine creates a numbing security. The work did not suit me but I found the people I worked with interesting. It was a first taste of grownup community. I admired the heroism of some who clearly were not happy in their work but endured it as a way to support their families.

When I told my managing director I was leaving to develop my career in journalism he looked at me with surprising admiration and envy. My future was thrillingly insecure. Making a living by the pen was very precarious but I was convinced of my gifts even if I didn't know what they were. I was ambitious to succeed, whatever success meant. Then I learned that Fr John had returned to his monastery in London and was setting up a lay community in which a small group of young laymen could

16

make a 6-month retreat meditating under his guidance. I went to see him to learn more and found him alone in a large house on the monastery grounds that he had just renovated. I made some joke about him being like a millionaire sitting alone on the top of his skyscraper. The idea of the lay community was attractive to me. It offered me the opportunity to master meditation, as I thought, and to prepare for my writing career. Fr John did not seem so sure it was right for me but after some repeated arguments to join he said yes.

The next 6 months were at various times gruelling, blissful, exciting and routine. I became caught by Fr John's vision of a 'community of love' as it seemed to offer both personal fulfilment and social change. It was the beginning of the global meditation community and, though I had no idea of this, the sense of being involved in something of ultimate importance was fulfilling in a way I had never felt before. I was never bored and I learned how easily one can waste life thinking that you are doing what you really want to do and trying to be free enough to achieve it. Two detached retinas and a month's convalescence unable to read introduced me to the tightrope the body walks constantly. Struggling with my addictions, smoking and thinking about myself, taught me the traps of my own mind and the need for guidance and support. Still, I was relieved when the 6 months were over and with my newfound self-knowledge and meditation practice I felt ready to go forth and do battle with the world for fame and fortune. Then to my great consternation I found that, somewhere in the last few months, I had lost my worldly ambition. For a young big ego it was like an older man discovering he had lost sexual desire.

Fr John listened sympathetically to my dilemma and encouraged me to leave anyway. As I struggled, he suggested I stay for another 6 months. I, however, wanted to make a big decision and a final, honest one. It was either the monastery in the queen of London's suburbs with my teacher, or the outside world full of promise and adventure. Trying to escape the looming idea of becoming a monk, I went to Italy where I had first learned the sensual arts. I made a diversion from them to visit Monte Cassino, the site of St Benedict's monastery, reconstructed after the war but now like a monastic theme park. One sweltering day I walked up the mountain to have a surly monk shut the door of the monastery in my face as it closed for lunch and siesta. Lying in the shade of the olive trees on the slopes beneath the monastery walls may have been the moment when I decided that I would go back and ask to become a novice and see where it led. An unexpected and unfamiliar peace began to fill my heart as the decision took shape.

What, then, is faith? I have said that faith is not belief. But we cannot define ourselves or anything about ourselves merely by a negation. What can we say positively about it?

Faith is multi-dimensional. It is a many-faceted action of the whole person. Every act of faith resonates with every aspect of the person responsible for it. Faith includes, integrates and expresses the person that I am, and who, of course I don't even fully understand. Actually, I can't fully understand myself except by being faithful, and as I become more faithful, I understand myself better. Self-knowledge leads me through transcendence of the person I thought I was and of the God I imagined to be God, to the knowledge of my true self in God. This process is not just a stage of development or a learning experience among others. It is the contextual meaning of existence repeated cyclically at ever deeper levels of reality. It is consummation of all existence, the return of the self to the source and our recapitulation into it by the source's own continuous act of love. Yet, even though self-knowledge is the process, we always remain a mystery to ourselves because our origin and our participation with this primal simple oneness of God is so subtle and boundless. Once we reach one frontier, another opens. I will always remain a mystery to myself, just as God is a mystery that no one knows fully except in the act of the divine self-knowing. We too are mystery because the depth of our being leads us to fall into the mystery of God. Falling in love, in human terms, is a very suggestive expression of the whole human enterprise. Falling itself doesn't demand faith but continuing into free fall does.

Faith is more than a statement, even one as risky as 'I love you'. It is an act of the whole person or, realistically, of the fragmented person moving into wholeness. 'Your faith has healed you,' Jesus said, 'Go in peace.' The faith of the blind beggar to whom Jesus spoke these words had merely told him what he wanted Jesus to do for him but his words came straight from the heart and expressed his whole self, his deepest desire.

Acts of faith, though, are not just one-off events. In the case of the beggar it initiated a new course of life. We make an act of faith incrementally. Little by little, day by day, redeeming our inevitable infidelities with forgiveness, humour, grace and then, yet again, renewed commitment. For anything significant we need to make daily acts of faith that are more than just good intentions, bargaining chips, ways of self-deception or mental games. The agent of these acts is our life itself, through sustained commitment to a person in marriage or friendship, to a chosen way of life, to a work, to a community, to a religion or to a spiritual discipline. They are acts of self-giving that are in themselves sacred and honourable and beautiful. Anyone who is attuned to them can recognize them even when they are performed in very different, parallel belief-systems. In making these acts we integrate ourselves. We become our selves and discover new potential and new aspects of our identity. Every act of faith in which we invest ourselves makes us more whole, more real, more self-aware, more conscious and more alive. In making any act of faith, we are also doing what Jesus meant by 'leaving self behind' because it is intrinsically transcendent. Leaving money, fame, power or pleasure behind is relatively easy compared with leaving self behind. For this we need another, something or someone outside ourselves. So we are obedient to the call of a teacher that makes us his disciples.

I said I would try to make this exploration of faith practical. Well, meditation is a very practical practice. Meditation is an act of faith. Meditating each day is a sustained way of faith. Every time we sit down to meditate, renouncing all the other options of that moment, the other things we could do or think about doing, the very act of sitting down and staying there for the duration is an act of faith. Deciding to give up the next 20 or 30 minutes in this unconditional way is an act of faith that is valid and effective even if the meditation seemed a waste of time and we sat through a storm of distraction and egocentricity. Saying the mantra, returning to the mantra throughout the time of the meditation, is an act of faith. At the heart of the practice is the deepest and most complete act of faith of which we are ultimately capable as human beings, to leave self behind. We do this not – as a merely belief-system religion might deduce – by anything penitential. Leaving self behind does not mean hurting oneself. Faith heals, it doesn't hurt. We do it by the simplest means known to human beings since the dawn of consciousness – by taking the attention off ourselves. By stopping thinking about ourselves.

Modern medical research illustrates the wisdom of the spiritual traditions for millennia that meditation is good for you. How that goodness is understood and measured varies according to your point of view. In this context I only want to say that meditation is good for you spiritually because it is a pure act of faith. Acts of faith are necessary for integrating our humanity. But for that very reason faith is more than just a drama of the moment, however heroic it might be, or even a series of repeated acts. It's also a process drawing its energy from and leading to a level of consciousness deeper than the one we started from. If it is true and deep, if it is really a leaving of self behind not just a performance we are enacting to feel good about ourselves or win admiration, faith opens up a new horizon for us, indeed an infinite series of horizons. Because it has a transcendent dynamic it takes our limits further – the limits of our identity are redrawn. Faith also pushes us into the future; it extends us in time because it is saying 'I am not controlled by what I am thinking or fearing at this instant'. Through faith we get a taste, en route, of the self that will one day be completed – in as much as it will be completed – when time is ended for us by the end of our spatial connection in the body. Anyone who has been and remained faithful despite fear, egotism and temptation thinks about time differently. They have a quietness about them that cannot be shaken by the crises of the moment. Faith alters our experience of time and we undergo time in a new way. Of course the clock still ticks and trains still have to leave on time with or without us but a new dimension of time has become conscious and within this new temporal existence ordinary time passes differently. The present moment becomes more palpably ever-present. The intersection of time and the present has been called tempiternity. It is a nice name with which to christen the child of faith.

*

This new sense of time awakened by faith is important and interesting when it comes to teaching meditation. After all, the reason most people give for not meditating is that they don't have the time for it.

I rarely meet people who disagree totally with meditation. There are occasionally those, usually religious people with a strong commitment to other forms of prayer, who become angry or condemnatory about meditation. Most people however trust the medical and scientific research about the benefits of meditation even if they don't listen to those teaching it from a spiritual tradition. (You are more likely to be advised to meditate by a therapist or a doctor than by a priest or minister.) But even among those who are convinced that meditation is a good thing many will say, 'I'd love to meditate every day but I just don't have time'. Yet, some of the busiest people in the world do make time; and by the 'busiest' people in the world, I'm thinking of a young mother who's got a job and four young children and makes the time to meditate as faithfully as she can. Or a managing director of a successful sovereign wealth fund. They would say that they can multitask in their busy lives better because they make the time to meditate. Many people meditate for purely therapeutic reasons especially to handle stress. Stress is simply the result of doing or imagining we have too much to do in the time available. Taking time not to *do* has a transforming influence on the experience of time.

However meditation, like faith itself, is not just an act squeezed into a busy schedule; it's an extension of an act, an extended action over time which becomes more significant and efficacious as time passes. Like marriage, monastic life or daily work faithfully performed, meditation is, as an element within them all, a way of faith that makes all the other aspects of our life more faithful (and consequently, as we will see, more loving as well). With strong, ever deepening, lifelong commitments such as to your family or work you are repeating day by day, moment by moment, the same act of faith that once got you started on this new path in your life. Making that path a way of faith changes you and by extension your life. Faith is an unfolding process. This takes time to become self-evident. When you begin meditation, for example, you might feel you are learning to master a difficult technique and you look for results that will justify your efforts. We have to be on guard against any kind of perfectionism or the wrong kind of measuring progress. But then one day you realize that you have now been meditating for several months or years and that you are no longer monitoring your progress and you are not resisting the discipline. Without having made you a saint it has changed you, worn away resistance and become a way of life enriching all aspects of your self.

At first, at the most superficial level, you might look at meditation and say,

> Oh, that's an interesting new way of prayer. It might help me feel more peaceful and calm as well as lowering my cholesterol. I'll give it a shot. Maybe the technique will speed up my spiritual growth or give me some nice new interesting experiences of God that I can talk or feel good about. I haven't had much spiritual experience for a while.

That's one way to begin. Maybe we all begin tentatively and conditionally to some degree. We feel our way on a new and unfamiliar path. But once we initiate that act of faith, however imperfectly (look at the very flawed disciples Jesus had to work with) it becomes a *way*, simply because we keep repeating that act of faith. We may not be able to say what we believe about meditation very clearly. When someone asks us why we meditate we may be embarrassed that we get tongue-tied and don't know what to say. The beliefs arise from the experience of faith and take form in their own time. Meditation itself, as I have said, is pure faith. We keep saying the mantra, we keep meditating day by day and then it opens up into something more than we had imagined. It becomes a process of self-knowledge sometimes painfully won as we encounter our shadow or confront our repressions and addictions. Yet it is a kind of self-knowledge distinct from the psychological insights we had before and which meditation will also lead to as a side-effect. It is the new, spirit-centred self-knowledge that changes us. It segues into the knowledge of God and yet we sense that we only know God because God knows us. And as self-knowledge grows it looks as if it is in fact God's knowledge of us. Rather odd. I know because I am known. On top of that interior experience the daily meditation also becomes a practice which subtly influences how we spend our time, our money and how we relate to our friends and the strangers who cross our path. Meditation requires set times yet we cannot separate it from everything else in our life. You can't compartmentalize it separately from the people you love or your marriage or family, your children or grandchildren or your community. Or from the way you respond to the news on the television or radio. Any way of faith reveals connections and relationships that we could not see before.

If meditation changes our life it's because it helps us to see the true value of living faithfully. It shows what being faithful in small things means, not just believing in big abstractions, or holding tenaciously to the comfort zone of certain ideas because we have always done so or because they shape an identity for us. As meditation develops the muscle of faith, integrity begins to matter more, not as a prescribed moral code but as a sense of what wholeness means. It is more uncomfortable living with ourselves if we act or speak without it, therefore we seek it even at some cost. Being a faithful human being, keeping our word, acting truly in all our relationships intimate and professional, trying to tell the truth as it is, being just and compassionate in small daily matters becomes increasingly linked to our sense of meaning. Faithful to what, we might ask. Just faithful, faithful in all we do – faithful in the way we love, faithful in the way we work, but faithful also in the way we walk and talk and walk the talk, faithful in the way we sit still in meditation, faithful in the way we accept the gift of life by using our time mindfully and treating our own body and others and our world with respect. In living faithfully we discover the meaning of goodness firsthand.

*

At the culmination of a Holy Week retreat on Bere Island in the south of Ireland about 30 of us we were standing together in the pure clear morning of Easter Sunday. We were loosely gathered around a large 'standing stone' of which there are many in that part of the world. It is a Neolithic monument, maybe 4,000 years old. No one knows exactly why it was put there – a marker, a memorial, a place of worship – but it is the spiritual and exact geographical centre of the island. It embodies stability, endurance and resilience. It has seen many sunrises and withstood many storms. We were there to wait for the Easter sun on a ravishingly beautiful morning, absolutely clear and mild, fresh and fragrant with just a few wisps of low-lying clouds over the hills and sea as if a painter had added them to the canvas for effect. An ancient Celtic belief is that the Easter day sun dances at dawn for sheer joy in the Resurrection. But we were not expecting that.

We arrived at about 6.15 in the morning. The sky was already bright but the sun had not yet risen. We realized it was going to take a while for the sun to rise because there is an important difference between dawn and sunrise. In fact, a difference at that time of the year of 45 minutes.

At the beginning of the long wait everybody was quite chatty and jokey and quite excited by the beauty and the sense of solidarity with each other. But as you can't keep that level up for very long people naturally fell to being quieter. There were longer periods of silence as we just looked ahead and allowed our senses to become more open. However delicious the moment, people also began hoping that the sun would rise soon so we could go off and have a nice breakfast. It was at that stage that, for me, it became a real parable of faith.

There were several aspects to it. First of all, there was an element of absolute certainty in it. That is, we knew the sun *was* going to rise, no doubt about that. Well, there was an infinitesimally faint chance that it might not rise. We live in a universe of probabilities. It might have been the last morning of the world and the end of everything. But it was unlikely. We knew it was going to happen, but the mind is a very strange thing even regarding (near) certainties. I had a flicker of doubt: maybe it wasn't going to rise or we were in the wrong place or maybe it rose earlier and we couldn't see it. The silly, foolish things that the mind says, which you have to notice and, if you are reasonably sane, you dismiss. As we were leaving later, someone remarked to me in a confidential tone that as the waiting had got longer he had an odd self-conscious anxiety. Maybe when the sun did actually arise it would be an anti-climax; he would feel disappointed and all the waiting would have seemed wasted time. So for him, and for others too perhaps, the excitement and drama of the wait, the expectation of fulfilment, declined. Anxiety grew with the feeling that you were even being cheated or fooled in some way. (We were mostly town people.) This was all related to the experience of time and empty stomachs. Faith is proven in and by time. As time passed the energy instilled by desire declined and a sense of confusion and disappointment raised the possibility of breaking faith. 'Blow this, let's go and have some eggs and bacon.'

We often long for something to happen. If it is true, as some philosopher once claimed, that the secret of happiness lies in a series of little treats, then anticipating them is part of the pleasure they give. Many would say that the desire is even more enjoyable than the consummation. You long for a week's holiday in a nice hotel in good company with good weather. The hotel is shabby, your companion has backache and the weather is awful. Desire is part of pleasure and can even be greater than its actual satisfaction. But you need the satisfaction even if it is not up to scratch, because if it goes on for too long, you give up the desire and look for something else to look forward to. Faith has an effect upon desire through the experience of time.

Then there was another aspect to our waiting around the standing stone. It was just the being together physically in each other's company. I think a few sent text messages to connect with people they wanted to be present to but that evidently is not the same as being physically together. Being in each other's presence, facing the same direction, which we literally were, eastwards, going through our inner weather while remaining turned towards each other, this is what community means. Friendship, a very pure form of love, is at the core of this and the waiting is a different experience when you wait together. We were making a collective act of faith by staying there. Some might have left had it not been for the energy and witness of their companions. So, even the endurance aspect of faith, perseverance, staying with it, hanging in there, reveals the nature of reality as relationship. Still, everybody had to make an individual decision to do that. Any one of us could have said, 'I've waited too long. I'm going back and have coffee'. The visible fact that we were all there made it easier for us all to stay together. If some had started to drift off it would have tested the faith of those who stayed. But it was more than an individual act of faith; there was something corporate about it as well. There was a *body of faith* that we were experiencing and faith grounds us in tradition, perhaps a specific ancient tradition that comes alive in a particular community of friends. Even that standing stone, for us therefore a place of worship, a sacred site, was a silent, moving symbol of a faithful dimension within humanity that extends back to the dawn of human consciousness.

Why did our ancestors erect these magnificent, silent and enigmatic monuments, the standing stones and stone circles, the burial sites aligned on the winter solstice, the wedge tombs in fields overlooking the sea? Like us they must have felt something of the tensions between certainty and probability. What meaning and satisfaction did they derive from their rituals at these places in communion with nature? We will never know what they believed. But we can feel that they had faith. The undiluted experience of faith always connects us with a tradition, a continuum existing within time, even unremembered time that is older than anything we can know about. Yet, however mysterious and intangible, it simultaneously embodies itself in an actual community of faith. This ancient faculty of faith was present here and now in this group of people, in this little band of people who came together for a Holy Week retreat, linked to a global network we call The World Community for Christian Meditation. This particular community of people here and now, or this centre or this small weekly meditation group connects us through the experience of faith to something universal in human nature.

*

A great transmission within its historical dimension in time manifests and takes shape in a particular community. The tradition is on a macro scale; the community is the micro scale. But they are really the same thing mirroring each other on different scales. As the Upanishads describe, the infinitely small and the infinitely great are the same thing. Or as the New Testament says, the Christ within us *is* the Cosmic Christ. To be connected experientially to that symmetry of scale is to be in the mystery of existence. Living in the mystery we find ourselves with changing perceptions of reality, including time. It changes the ways we see; and it changes the direction in which we are looking.

*

So, an act of faith integrates us as a person. Integration always awakens a sense of depth and mystery. Faith is both a transcendence and a real-time commitment. We leave self behind; that is transcendence. We transcend our isolated individuality as we commit ourselves to the whole, the unity in which we are an indivisible part. But integration comes at a cost. We have to make many hard, daily choices in preparation for the eventual great choiceless choice of our full awakening. Do I stay and wait for the sun to rise or do I go back and have a coffee? Do I sit and meditate this evening or watch a movie? Until the mystery of integration is consummated a choice *for* is always, painfully, a choice *against* something else.

Commitment to anything – a relationship, a marriage, study, a work or cause, a spiritual practice – depends upon a personal giving of self that is extended over time. It therefore de-prioritizes the pleasure-principle. Usually we are trained to do what we want to do, immediately or as soon as possible. 'I want breakfast now!' Faith extended through time, also renewing itself by means of the infidelities by which it grows, develops self-control. Not the most glamorous or obviously heroic of virtues, self-control is nevertheless an indispensable element of all creativity and heroic achievement.

If we are living by faith, then, we may say, 'Breakfast is a good thing to want and to have. I'm really going to enjoy it but I'm going to defer that pleasure until the sun rises'. There is a discipline, a self-learning, in that. There is also an *ascesis*, a training exercise, in it. Saying not yet (or not so much) doesn't mean we don't enjoy breakfast or can't find sensual and intellectual pleasure in things. It means we are not being controlled by the compulsion for instant gratification and thus we learn patience. One of the fruits of meditation, patience is also one of the fruits of the Holy Spirit. This means it is a way of living rather than a skill we perfect and show off. Patience expresses a new and more serene relationship to time, a new way of *being*, in time.

Our patience was rewarded and the doubts some had that it would be anticlimactic were forgotten in the glory of the sunrise. The golden disc rose above the mountain top like a baby's head appearing at childbirth. It pushed upward as a pure force of nature, serene, irrepressible, pulsating with life. Entirely itself and entirely natural. The world was beautified in its golden, generous radiance. The dancing was all within us who were there and who had waited in faith.

John Main again:

Meditation is the prayer of faith because we have to leave our selves behind before the other appears and without the pre-packaged guarantee that the other will appear. (*Word into Silence*, p. 21)

3

The Power of Faith

Thinking that my life as a monk would unfold in the suburbs of west London, where the monastery was located with its parish and school, and being assured privately by some of the monks that I might in the distant future become headmaster, made me readjust my expectations of life. For the time being I was very content. Life, as always in a monastery, was busy. My friends thought I was spending the day walking a cloister with my hood up avoiding eye contact. In fact the day was regulated between meditation, the Office and Mass and my jobs in the monastery, library, sacristy and whatever else I was asked to do. As a novice I was the lowest in the hierarchy. Surprisingly, I relished the freedom this gave me. Above all, I was working closely with Fr John and seeing with wonder the teaching of meditation spread.

One of his gifts was to know when to let go and jump. Although he was personally stable and integrated – or because he was – his life was punctuated by surprise renunciations and radical new beginnings. At his prompting the monastery accepted the invitation he had from the Archbishop of Montreal to start a small Benedictine community for teaching meditation; it was agreed that I would go with him and do my theology there rather than in Rome. As we were leaving the house in London for the airport, being driven by one of the monks, I remembered I had left my shirts and socks behind and dashed back in to put them in the first bag to hand. Thus, as we arrived in Montreal in pouring rain lugging suitcases and carrying plastic bags we were starting another both phase of our life and perhaps a new form of the monastic tradition of the desert. The bishop was there to welcome us and show us the house he had acquired for us – a charming old Quebec farm-house house – stranded by history in the city, which became but didn't look like a monastery.

Our monastic form of life was cut back to the simple essentials, prayer, community, work and study, but it was more real. Over the next 5 years the community expanded and the outreach began that was later to form the 'monastery without walls'. The old personal struggles with the ego never ceased but I had never been happier. Then, far too soon, the shadow of death began to approach.

After his operation for colon cancer Fr John was pronounced cured. By early 1982, new treatment became necessary and it became clear the cancer was unstoppable. I saw him adapt and accept. He dived into the mystery of living and dying and his teaching and our relationship deepened accordingly. On the brink a strange peace can be found. One afternoon we sat talking about the future. I asked him what I should do. The work was growing, but as a community we were small and fragile. I didn't feel at all ready to take over. He looked straight at me and with a tender smile simply said 'you'll do what you have to do'. It made me feel both abandoned and invisibly, intangibly held.

During his last weeks the shadow of death grew stronger. But in his company the light at times became blinding. I felt the cold shadow, fear and loss, only away from his physical presence. With him, the energy of life as love became more intense and the joy stronger. We were living the teaching, hardly speaking about it. When he stopped breathing the world stopped, and didn't stop. I knelt beside the empty body and a huge impersonal emptiness poured into me and exploded.

THE POWER OF FAITH

This is also from John Main:

> The essence of all poverty consists in the risk of annihilation. This is the leap of faith from ourselves to the other. This is the risk involved in all loving. (*Word into Silence*, p. 21)

I said above that faith is an act. It's not something we just think about. It's not an ideal or a concept. It's something we live and dramatize. In time we may even come to embody it as well. It is an act extended in the dimension of time. The degree of its extension, meaning how long we are faithful, is a measure of the power of faith. It is this power of faith that makes things happen and changes us.

Jesus said that even a small measure of faith, the size of a mustard-seed, can move a mountain. Let's not take him too literally. We can understand this in terms of psychological blocks, for example, an addiction or compulsion or other negative patterns of behaviour such as violence or anger. Faith can bring change where we had despaired of ever changing. Even to accept what cannot be improved is a change. Faith heals, as many healing stories in the gospels remind us, and faith leads to spiritual vision. 'Faith is the vision of things unseen' as the 'Letter to the Hebrews' puts it.

If somebody says to you 'I'll be faithful to you for – well, at least the rest of today', that doesn't exactly thrill us. Faith needs to be extended and it is extended and tested in time through repetition. That is faithful living. It confronts our appetite for novelty, in sexual, gastronomic or geographical senses. We like secure patterns of life – getting the same train to the same office every day. And yet we long to break out of these repetitive patterns and be free. We take holidays but wouldn't really want to be on holiday all the time. Many people live lives of quiet desperation because they feel trapped in mechanical patterns of repetition and have never found a way of repeating the same thing faithfully. Some surrender into a deadening routine because it offers security even at the cost of vitality.

Faith involves choice and choice means that we prioritize. The temptation or inclination to break out of a commitment is never far away. It can be calmly sublimated or it can rage and lead us to destroy a good life and loving relationships. To regress to a pre-choice moment, to the plethora of choice in adolescence, is to revert to a choice that we once rejected. A man can come home one day after 20 years of marriage and announce that he is leaving. A woman who has made a home for her family for 20 years can go and get a part-time job for the first time and promptly fall in love with her new boss and abandon husband and family. Faith is not a prison or security compound we construct for ourselves to prevent this sort of thing happening. This temptation can strike at any time as the history of broken hearts can testify.

*

Faith is a way – a way of life, a way of behaving over time – by which we give. But if we see it as only giving, only as commitment and sacrifice, we will find it hard to grow in the many ways that faith enables us to become more fully human. We will only see the hard side of faith not the bright side. Because in faith, we also receive. There is this mutuality of exchange in faith because it is a personal act that enhances our entire personal experience. It's not just cold objectivity; it's warm inter-subjectivity. It brings us into deeper relationship with others. Part of this mutuality may mean being put to the test. Often we test the faith that we feel has been put in us: *How much do you really love me? If you really saw me at my worst you'd withdraw – so here, see the monster I really am.* Perhaps we are only convinced that someone has put their faith in us when they freely lay down their life for us. Maybe – from a psychological point of view – this also applies in the ground of all relationship to God as well. The laying down of our lives for each other in love is the consummation of a significant act of faith. We may believe in God but it's always harder to believe that God believes in us.

Faith is process and this process comes to shape and give character to the personality. There are people we know whom we recognize as faithful people, faithful in the promises they make and above all remaining faithful to us through difficult times. Such people are usually friendly and well thought of and yet curiously detached and expectant. They are dependable and they keep loving in the midst of conflict or temptation. We feel blessed to have such people in our lives or even to have met them in passing. They are recognizable. But we also know people who are unfaithful, not by malice but because they are simply unable to commit or to be constant. They are weak and often know that about themselves. They try, but then forget what they promised, or surrender to the latest mood. We are quick to judge others, but who knows what others might really think about us? Either way, in faith or in infidelity, by its presence or absence, faith is a moral shaping force in our life; it expresses and determines our moral behaviour.

Some time ago Britain found itself in the grip of a political crisis because it had been revealed that many of its members of parliament had been working the system to give themselves excessive expenses, claiming for the cleaning of their moats or killing of moles in their gardens or for second homes that were fake. Ordinary people were outraged and the media had a field day. The outrage was moral. Everyone had made jokes about the untrustworthiness of politicians before but the extent and pettiness of this scandal made people everywhere feel let down by a whole system in which they still had some trust – because we have to believe in something – and feel betrayed and disillusioned. Maybe people felt even a little scared that those with elected responsibility were behaving so badly. What more were they concealing from us? One of the defences many MPs made was that in making their claims they had been 'acting in good faith'. They admitted their mistakes and would pay back what they had pilfered but at the time they thought they were acting morally. Most people didn't believe that. It gave extra passion to people who said, 'Oh no, you weren't. You were acting in bad faith, and this is a betrayal of the faith we put in you'.

The meaning of faith is an important determining factor not only for our personal, spiritual lives but for the quality of our socio-political life and the integrity of our culture. Civilization ultimately rests upon faith. The banking scandals that lie behind the great recession of the second decade of this century expose this graphically. The banking system had to be rescued at huge expense because it is needed to run a modern society, and banking, we are often reminded, runs on trust. But what happens when a whole profession or major institutions in society become unfaithful? Political corruption in many Third World societies shows us. The cancer of corruption metastases and growth and social development are arrested. The poor get poorer while the rich get greedier. We learn by imitation and if we see people acting unfaithfully (fathers, politicians, bankers) we learn to live by the same murky standards and come to feel or at least to convince ourselves that they are normal. Because the fingers of the men at the top are sticky why shouldn't I, too, even at the bottom of the pile, screw my bit out of those weaker than me?

The meaning of faith is taught and inherited. If not, we corrupt the young and bring about our own destruction. This is why it is so important to be concerned about the quality of faith by which we operate.

*

Bede Griffiths said that faith is our capacity for transcendence. This means that it's our ability to go beyond the ego and the self-centred priorities that our ego blindly advances and defends. Faith is our capacity to re-centre ourselves in another, in someone we love, in a person in need, and consequently in

God who is the otherness in which we lose and find ourselves. By faith we find our true centeredness, our balance and our wholeness.

Like other human capacities this capacity for transcendence takes time to develop. We don't expect children or adolescents to have it fully developed. We make allowances for inexperience and youthful mistakes. But it doesn't only take time. It also requires will-power. You have to want to develop it. You have to have some small insight into what it means and why it is important for human development. You also need to have the personal, the communal, the cultural reinforcement and support for this process of developing it. Faith grows and it is a measure of our growth as a whole person and as a citizen.

St Paul understood this as he watched and guided the early Christians. He planted the seed of the gospel way of life among them, by word and example. Then he had to leave them to grow it themselves. When he saw them drifting back to their old ways dominated by fear, superstition and escapist desire he strongly called them back. In a passage like this we can see what faith meant to him:

> Before this faith came, we were close prisoners in the custody of the law, pending the revelation of faith. The law was a kind of tutor in charge of us until Christ should come, when we should be justified through faith; and now that faith has come, the tutor's charge is at an end. For through faith you are all children of God in union with Christ Jesus . . . there is no such thing as Jew and Greek, slave and free, male and female; for you are all one person in Christ Jesus. (Gal. 3:23–29)

Here we see that faith is more than belief. It is choice to be and to remain free. Just believing something doesn't make all this happen. We also see in this experience of spiritual community that faith is and operates in more than a psychological reality.

True, our spiritual growth is effected in our psychological experience in the way that mind is reflected in brain chemistry. But they are not the same thing. Faith in Christ doesn't just make us feel better through the release of endorphins. It realizes our oneness with all other beings, regardless of social or even gender differences. Faith achieves such a high dividend because it evolves into love. An early Church Father taught this shortly before he died as a martyr for the faith he held.

> Of all these things none is hidden from you if you are single-hearted and if you direct your faith and love toward Jesus Christ. These are the beginning and the end of life: the beginning is faith, the end is love. The two bound together in unity are God. Everything else that belongs to goodness follows from these. No one who professes faith sins, and anyone who possesses love does not hate. The tree is known by its fruit. (Ignatius of Antioch, 'To the Ephesians')

Faith grows and bears fruit; it grows through trial, even death and certainly through daily temptation. Crucially – if we are to avoid the dangers of perfectionism – it also grows through failure and forgiveness. The spiritually-oriented person is not a perfect person. Everyone is unfaithful at times, in thought, word or deed. But the spiritually-active person continually makes the growth process a matter of high priority and this turns failure, infidelity around.

This doesn't mean we separate faith-development from the other aspects of our lives in which faith is practiced. That would be phoney religion of the most anaemic kind. An artist does not confuse the studio with the work he is doing, or a musician the instrument with the music played. They are simultaneously distinct and inseparable: just like faith and the responsibilities and realities of life. Work, family and relationships are the laboratory. We cannot claim to be faithful in family life and lie and cheat at work, or be faithful to a spouse, but exploit the poor.

THE POWER OF FAITH

Faith is an unfolding of the core identity of the human person. It is a central value, a central, constellating aspect of our whole human development. In whatever we are doing at work, in our personal relationships, in family life, in our responsibilities to the marginalized, we are putting this quality of faith to work at the very centre of our life. In every act of faith we turn towards another more fully. If we turn to one person in this way we turn to all. Transcendence of self thus leads to growth in love and onwards to the ultimate goal that is union with God, the ultimate other in whom all selves meet, and powerhouse of love.

*

For growth there needs to be a consistency between the three levels of our self where faith is active. The physical level is the field of action – just do it. Mentally, we need to understand why we are doing it and what it really means. Here we formulate and test the right beliefs expressed as accurately as we can. I have said we should not confuse faith and belief. Nevertheless faith needs to be conscious and so will always be related to beliefs, the attempts we make to understand, to conceptualize, and express the meaning of faith and what we are putting our faith in. This is needed if faith is to open the third level, the spiritual dimension. So, intellectually, philosophically, theologically, we need to understand as clearly as we can. In dialogue with tradition and with new fields of knowledge we need to find and test the beliefs and doctrines that we live by. A healthy tradition capable of transmitting itself to a new generation has belief and faith in harmony.

Holding beliefs with integrity doesn't mean that what I believe necessarily contradicts what you believe just because they different. Dialogue, respect and reverence for other's beliefs are more than tolerance although they form a mark of a just and civilized society or religion. We should seek to identify and understand the truth in others' beliefs and then treat them with the same reverence we give our own even while we remain with our own. We may feel that in my tradition I find the best beliefs by which to strengthen and express my experience of faith. And, without being bigoted or trying to convert others, we may also believe that our tradition is objectively the best, the most clear, comprehensive and inclusive expression of faith. However we may value our own tradition, if our beliefs express faith but don't try to substitute for it, we will not condemn others for believing differently or force them to change. Even if we feel our tradition is the highest expression of truth we will also know that truth can never be imposed. If our attachment to it makes it into a cause of conflict it ceases to be the truth we started out with. Faith may make us die for the truth but it will not allow us to be violent or dishonest in the cause of truth. Where faith is active, dialogue replaces conflict and mutual curiosity replaces condemnation.

In trying to understand our beliefs, we will only ever achieve limited success. But hitting our limit – and recognizing it when we do – is a notable achievement. We are meant to come to this limit of our intellectual understanding because this is the point where the contemplative consciousness awakens. '*We can never know God by thought, only by love*' as *The Cloud of Unknowing* says, or as St Augustine put it concisely: '*If you can understand it, it isn't God.*'

Touching the limits of our intellectual and emotional understanding of God may at first feel like failure. They are frustrating, as all limitations are, especially if we put all our eggs in one cerebral-emotional basket. A higher intelligence needs to be listened to that says that coming to this frontier is a real spiritual achievement and the beginning of a new stage of our development. The darkness of faith at this stage is simply the failure of the mind to conceptualize. Even if beliefs and feelings seem to falter and confuse at this stage – as they will – the way of faith will see us through.

*

Take the Eucharist for example. Catholic tradition, in particular, makes an extraordinary claim about this ritual and over the centuries has come up with a rich range of beliefs to try to explain it. But even if we don't occupy our minds with these doctrines intellectually we can still participate in the Mass profitably. We can get something out of it emotionally and we may feel better for having gone. But what happens if this emotional, devotional satisfaction is withdrawn? Maybe it's because we don't like the way it is celebrated or because we are taking stock of ourselves and realize the Mass has become too mechanical and uninteresting and we just cannot see beyond that emotional downer. So we stop going to Mass for a while. Or, we may continue in blind faith, hoping and groping our way while our beliefs are being reviewed and updated. During this period we may even feel that we have 'lost our faith' while in fact our faith as such has never been stronger. This is much more likely to be the case if we are also sustained by a contemplative practice that gives us an experience of interior presence which seeks for an external, sacramental expression. In time, as faith and beliefs are rebalanced, we find that the Eucharist has taken on a new and deeper, mystical meaning. Then even a series of boring sermons doesn't throw us off.

The spiritual dimension is entered through faith. Faith leads to the 'vision of things unseen'. It verifies the existence of realities invisible to the conceptual and visual mind alone. This contemplative experience of spiritual vision is a fruit of the life of faith. It opens up a new sense, a more subtle spiritual sense in which we are able to register and recognize patterns, presences, associations that before we were unable to perceive.

Psychologically, this whole process is very fruitful. At first the shadow side, long repressed and avoided, may bubble up and even flood us at times. But we also experience personal growth and healing through the self-transcendence that we develop through faith. We may not be the first to recognize these changes. The people who know us well or with whom we live and work may point something out to us and we quietly realize that, yes, we are changing. Not perfected yet, perhaps, but as we move beyond orbit of the ego, we see ourselves growing in our capacity for love, for empathy, for wisdom and moderation. As this happens the fruits of faith take on deeper meaning – not just as psychological benefits but as signs of the divine life expanding and transforming us. If people say that meditation makes their lives more meaningful it is not because it whispers the secrets of the riddles of the universe in our ear. But because we sense that our ultimate destiny is coming into clearer focus within the ordinary round of our daily lives. We see that we are designed to be divinized. We feel the gratitude that any experience of grace brings. Traditionally, we say faith is a gift of grace. This means we are both surprised and enriched by something we could never claim to deserve. We begin to see what faith really means.

The ego is quietened and tamed by this insight. We don't feel proud at this growth that is happening through faith because we recognize that it is gift and that it is the work of love in us beyond our understanding. Yet the same faith that allows us to see further than the mind's reach can itself be seen. Jesus 'saw the faith' of the woman with the haemorrhage whom he healed. He saw the faith of Bartimaeus, the blind beggar. He also saw the lack of faith in his closest disciples.

4

Stages of Faith: Purgation

No work of wisdom better describes the nuances of the cycle of growth and decline than the Chinese classic the I Ching, *the 'book of changes'. Calibrating the conscious and unconscious mind, bringing chance and will into relationship, the hexagrams ask to be read and understood. Like the parables of the* New Testament, *we get what we can from them according to our capacity. Life is seen to be in constant evolution. Things rise to a climax of fullness and then begin to decline until they hit the lowest point. The* I Ching *– and indeed any teaching of faith – urges us above all to avoid denying the cyclical nature of things. False optimism or despair await us that route. Instead we are told to listen, to recognize the subtle shifts in the unfolding of our lives and to adjust our responses according to the direction things are moving. The problem is that we have to learn on the job. Mistakes are inevitable and necessary, though we can go some way to mitigating them and doing damage control.*

Returning to the monastery after Fr John's funeral was – as anyone who has experienced bereavement can remember – like returning to an empty tomb. Except it wasn't empty: there was a community, weekly meditation groups, visitors and a daily schedule of prayer, meals, housecleaning and garden maintenance. All one can do at times is the next thing that has to be done. Fr John's advice to me was right. I had no sure idea where we were going. Many thought it was a matter of time before the priory collapsed. With a combination of faith and ego we were all determined with youthful energy to keep going and not give up before we had to. I did not know the I Ching at this time but I imagine this is what it would serenely have advised.

The first sign that we were not just surviving but growing – and there's no life without growth – came from the meditators outside the walls but quite clearly no less within the community. Visitors from Singapore, England, the United States, other cities in Canada, Australia – one after another indicated that the seed had scattered and found fertile soil. Although the monastic community struggled for its identity – as they all do – it was on its foundation that the monastery without walls began to develop. I travelled more, the community needed more and the secret of meeting all requirements remained elusive. A tension grew between the inner and the outer dimensions of the community. Too much was projected globally upon the small local community and it did not have the privacy or time to itself that it needed. It is easier to reflect on this in retrospect than it was at the time to deal with it. Increasingly the tension of building a young monastic community and sustaining a global outreach became more acute and I certainly made mistakes that I hope I would be able to avoid now. I remembered how my mother, soon after I had become a monk, expressed surprise that there could be such things as disputes in monasteries. Well, the Rule of St Benedict is largely about handling them. They may look slight to the outsider because so much of the monastic life is protected from the problems of the world. But for this very reason they can be the more intense and inescapable. Anyone who has gone through hard times in a marriage, and most married couples have, will understand the peculiar and very deep anxiety such domestic and interior suffering creates.

I had resigned as prior and stopped in London after a visit to Asia when I heard abruptly that the priory was closed. It was another death. It felt worse because it could all have been handled better; much could have been avoided even saved, but the factuality of death speaks for itself. All of us involved, monks, *oblates and meditators worldwide felt the shock waves. Those closest to the epicentre suffered the worst. We had hit the nadir, the lowest point of the cycle. The stone rolled against the mouth of the tomb seemed to me unbudgeable. I returned to London and again tried to be faithful, not to a great vision that seemed to have been shattered but just to the next ordinary thing each morning and evening that simply needed to be done.*

The classical understanding of this *process* of faith in the mystical theology of the Christian tradition sees it as the stages of purgation (purification), illumination (enlightenment) and union. We will now take a look at these three phases of spiritual development.

Each act of faith initiates a process that is potentially extendable into the unknown future. Faith has a momentum of its own. It pushes us onwards to places that we would never have thought of going to or perhaps never have chosen. But any sincere commitment makes us feel impelled to keep on this way of faith to the end – if possible. With experience we learn, let's hope so anyway, to be cautious about what we put our faith in and what we promise to do. Through our failures and infidelities we come to know the shame and the self-disappointment of breaking faith. Infidelity does not make us feel good about ourselves, however we may justify it or even, on occasions, how understandable it may be. When a marriage breaks down, for example, and separation is the only healthy solution, however necessary it is, no one feels good about it. A commitment to be faithful has broken down.

Religious groups offer marriage preparation to their young members and most young couples today move in with each other to try out life together before making a formal commitment. St Benedict encourages the novice to think carefully about his commitment to the monastic life. He gives him a year to discern and assigns wise older monks to advise him. (This preparation for final vows has now been extended to three or more years.) Then, if he does decide to enter, he must realize it is all the way, for life. But even then after this solemn moment of commitment the journey is just beginning:

> We are, therefore, about to found a school of the Lord's service, in which we hope to introduce nothing harsh or burdensome. But even if, to correct vices or to preserve charity, sound reason dictates some hard discipline, do not at once fly

in dismay from the way of salvation, the beginning of which cannot but be narrow. But as we advance in the religious life and faith, we shall run the way of God's commandments with expanded hearts and unspeakable sweetness of love; so that never departing from His guidance and persevering in the monastery till death, we may by patience share in the sufferings of Christ, and be found worthy to be coheirs with Him of His kingdom. (Prologue – The Rule of Benedict)

The act of faith is more like boarding a plane than disembarking at your destination. St Paul, at the beginning of the letter to the Romans, says that salvation is a way of faith; it begins in faith and it ends in faith. That is, it is an open-ended process. Similarly, John Main reminds us that more rather than less faith is needed to make the journey of meditation. There is no final graduation ceremony for faith, no diploma to put on your wall. In the course of its journey we are told that we will undergo many changes, not least concerning the way we understand what the journey itself is about. It all has an unbendable single-mindedness about it because every act of faith is like shooting an arrow and arrows don't meander. They have a single direction. The relentless deepening of faith comes in time to mirror God's tenacious love for us. Once hooked, we cannot escape it. Not surprisingly then, any faith journey – meditation, marriage or other personal commitments – can be exciting at first but also, at crucial moments of growth, a bit scary.

*

Purgation, the first purifying stage, can be felt strongly at times in the early days of learning to meditate. It is many things going on at once including a cleansing of memory. A good account of this is the story of St Anthony of the Desert.

He became a monk at a young age after having been pierced to the heart by the words of Jesus he heard spoken in church to 'go and sell everything you have and come follow me'. Anthony was a wealthy young man and heard these words addressed directly to himself. He accomplished this renunciation in two stages. He had given away most of his wealth but retained some of it to look after his sister, but, when the absolute nature of the call dawned on him, he gave away even her portion too and put the girl in a convent. We don't know what she felt about this. But the detail is meant to show that at first we try to get away with a less than total gift of self. He then went into his first stage of the desert life. The subsequent stages of his life were to be marked by ever-deeper plunges into solitude in the desert. The purgative stage of his life was prolonged. At the age of 35, perhaps his mid-life crisis and at the age when Jung says all questions in life become spiritual issues, he decided to isolate himself in an abandoned fort.

He asked friends to bring him bread and water. However self-denying his decisions may seem to us, they were not self-destructive. In fact, the way they are described is intended to emphasize how moderate he was compared with some of the monastic crazies around at the time. St Athanasius, his biographer, tells us that his work of radical *ascesis*, of spiritual training and purification, continued for the next 20 years. Eventually, his friends thought they'd better check out what had happened to him. Perhaps they were prepared for the worst, a physically decrepit man prematurely aged and demented. They were in for a surprise and this, rather than the graphic details of self-denial, is the point of the story.

We are told that he came forward to greet them smiling. He was neither too fat for want of exercise, nor too thin for lack of food. He had a radiant complexion, his eyes sparkling, his mind clear and rational, healthy in body, in mind and in spirit, free in his detachment from the fears and desires of the ego, the fear of rejection, the desire for approval. The only physical defect we are told about is that his teeth had been worn down by the dry bread that had been his main diet. His example inspired many to follow him and he is revered as the founder of Christian monasticism.

> Antony, as from a shrine, came forth initiated in the mysteries and filled with the Spirit of God. Then for the first time he was seen outside the fort by those who came to see him. And they, when they saw him, wondered at the sight, for he had the same habit of body as before, and was neither fat, like a man without exercise, nor lean from fasting and striving with the demons, but he was just the same as they had known him before his retirement, And again his soul was free from blemish, for it was neither contracted as if by grief, nor relaxed by pleasure, nor possessed by laughter or dejection, for he was not troubled when he beheld the crowd, nor overjoyed at being saluted by so many. But he was altogether even as being guided by reason, and abiding in a natural state. Through him the Lord healed the bodily ailments of many present, and cleansed others from evil spirits. And He gave grace to Antony in speaking, so that he consoled many that were sorrowful, and set those at variance at one, exhorting all to prefer the love of Christ before all that is in the world. (The Life of St. Antony Athanasius)

He invites comparison – were one to take the story literally in all details – Henri Charriere, the hero of *Devil's Island* and the book and film *Papillon,* whose many years of incarceration and abuse had not dimmed his desire to be free. But in the Athanasius version of the legend – a theological statement – it was not only his mind but his body that were actually enhanced, brought to full health, by his years of *ascesis.* The sequel is vitally important to understanding the story. All this *ascesis* was only the beginning of Anthony's real work, his service in the world for others. He had found his true self in God and was now stabilized in his 'natural state'. Henceforth, we are told, he gave himself over to the four great ways of service to others: teaching, healing the sick, reconciling those divided by conflict and giving comfort to the sorrowful.

Making allowance for the intention of the storyteller we can still see in this archetypal description of the spiritual journey a useful parable about its meaning for us in our very different circumstances. The story illustrates the essential Christian idea that the work of contemplation is a work of love and can only be fully judged by the love that it produces. Nor is there is anything morbid about the first difficult stage of the spiritual journey, however long the purification process may last. There is no indication from Anthony that the body or physical desire is being punished, no sense that we are trying to repress or destroy any part of ourselves or even to lacerate our ego. The pain is seen as therapeutic. His ego and his body became healthier because of his self-discipline. Simplification – even though more radical than most of us feel drawn to – not pain was his way to this new health. This illustrates faith as a means of healing, a way of coming to wholeness. We then also see how real, hard-won holiness is automatically placed at the service of others.

*

St Athanasius' biography of Anthony goes into some graphic detail, a Jungian dream, about the ordeals he passed through in order to come to this calm and compassionate mind. His 'temptations' became the inspiration for many works of art in later centuries from Bosch to Dali. Most of them emphasize the erotic temptations, but the account itself highlights purification of motive and the transcendence of ego. Purgation is hard but natural, unavoidable and life-giving as we experience also in meditation. It is a cleansing of the memory. We too have to face the dead, to see through the ghosts of our past and look at them without being scared to death by them. In the same batch we have to face our dead or archived selves, our dormant attachments, repressed fears and guilts and above all the losses we have endured. We have to look them in the eye because there is no other way of being free from their influence and completely updating, refreshing ourselves into the present. Sometimes on the internet you go to a favourite homepage and notice that nothing has changed since you last visited. If you click the 'refresh page' things go whirling in cyberspace and when the page reappears you see the latest, updated version. To be alive and enjoy our freedom we have to stop living in the past and to get updated. We have to break with the habits that keep us controlled by our personal history or cultural conditioning. A re-patterning of ourselves happens through a combination of our own efforts, sustained by faith, and of grace which will surely reach us eventually if we stay faithful to the process.

Adapt yourselves no longer to the pattern of this present world but let your minds be remade and your whole nature thus transformed. (Rom. 12:2)

To achieve this, we need to take off our shoes as we enter the holy ground of the present moment. Moses found God one day in a bush that was burning without its own fuel. This describes nicely the present moment. He was told by God from the bush to take off his shoes because he was standing on holy ground. Early commentaries of this command explain that he took off his leather sandals, made of dead skin that separated him from direct contact with the holy ground of reality. This reconnection to direct experience is what happens in meditation as we lay aside memories as the best way to purify them. It is not a one-off technique or even a course like a 10day antibiotic course but a process that we come to follow more and more as a way of faith. As the preconceptions and attachments that distort a direct perception of reality fall away through the laying aside of thoughts we re-relate to everything directly. The labels that we've stuck

51

on things, the price-tags and the name-tags peel off. We feel it at the time as a loss but it is a prelude to finding something.

In the stage of purgation, we often feel anxious as the conventional naming system in which we have been conditioned gets shaken and even begins to feel redundant. Religious people often feel they are 'losing their faith' just when their faith has begun to grow, perhaps for the first time in years. Most real change at first feels like loss.

That's why it's sad when you hear of people going through a tough, purifying stage of meditation and who go to a spiritual director who doesn't have much personal knowledge of the contemplative experience. When the director hears the person say they feel dry, discouraged by the lack of progress, or that the mantra feels like a distraction, they jump to the wrong diagnosis and suggest the wrong remedy. They may say, 'Give it up! It's not working for you, try something else!' Personal experience of the stages is an essential qualification for giving advice about them. The more experienced one is, the less prescriptive advice one is likely to give. Instead, one is going to be gentler in the more empathic encouragement to persevere. We need to hear this from each other when we feel deeply discouraged. This is why spiritual friendship rather than spiritual direction is the better way of understanding what we give to each other on the contemplative path. There are times we can see only the 'thick cloud' which Moses entered to meet God and then, it is good to feel the squeeze of a friendly hand.

*

In meditation, the purifying process gives us a kind of anonymity. We may feel that we're losing our own name. *Who am I,* after all? As we feel ourselves changing we can't answer this question so readily. It even becomes a frightening question at some moments as our social personality is called into doubt. We find ourselves in a strange country without a passport or papers and we are not yet aware that we are citizens of heaven. But then – using now the language of the book of Revelation – if we prove victorious, God will give us 'some of the hidden manna' and 'a white stone with a new name written on it known only to the person who receives it'. Perseverance, faith, is 'rewarded'.

This moment of renaming, feeling ourselves updated in our true identity, may be a *satori* moment, a spontaneous enlightenment experience. For the Zen practitioner this is a crucial test of progress and the master has to validate it as genuine. But for the Christian, the focus is different and the test of faith is not made on individual enlightenment experiences. They come to any real practitioner, of course, from time to time, but in the Christian way of faith we are not looking for them; nor are we judging our meditation by the intensity or the frequency of these enlightenment moments. We are rather putting our emphasis upon the growth in faith which is tested and verified by our expanding capacity for love.

The purgative stage is about re-programming, letting go, shedding our self-rejection, doubts and the feelings of unworthiness that stick to us like velcro. All of these states of mind impede or block progress because they make us identify ourselves with the prison of our limitations. As we push the horizon back we see that the whole process of faith is about learning that we are loved. We find out that no belief system can save us but that faith heals us. And that faith active in love saves and liberates.

The purifying power of this stage of faith is attention, pure attention. We are in fact giving and sustaining our attention to the good in ourselves, the natural goodness at the core of our being. This is not, what it may sound like, becoming self-centred and self-obsessed with our spiritual success. The sign that it is not self-fixation is simply recognized: it awakens us to the essential goodness in other people, even those who have harmed us, and to the sheer goodness at the heart of the world. 'God saw all that he had made and saw that it was very good.'

Keeping our attention on the good, even in times when all we can feel is toxic and hopeless; this is the work of faith. Attention purifies. The mantra is the work of pure attention and the simple faith needed to say it teaches us very simply and directly what faith means. The work of purification becomes simpler and even easier when we understand that our power of attention is nothing less than the attention that we ourselves are receiving. Our capacity to give attention is equal to the attention that we are being given at the deepest centre of our being. No one has anything to give they have not received. Knowing this is poverty of spirit.

This realization may grow slowly, or at times hit us like a ton of bricks. Understanding it marks a transition from the purgative stage to the unfolding of the next, the beginning of the illuminative stage. The purgation goes on of course throughout life, but the emphasis shifts from the purifying, purgatorial fire in which the ego's desires and fears are consumed, to the transforming influence of the light of Christ.

*

In this first stage of faith, the purification process triggers a cleansing of memories we no longer thought we had.

It is like cleaning your room after many months or doing an annual spring-clean. It is surprising to see how much you have accumulated and kept which you should have tossed away long ago. As in starting to meditate you first feel very enthused about the process and even if at first you delay doing it seriously and find all kinds of good excuses not to, eventually you get down to it. And, of course, it's about *your* home; it's something *you* know *you* have to do. You can't just get a cleaner in to do it for you because only you know exactly what you can throw away, what you have to keep and where you like things to be.

There is a moment in the journey of faith when we feel prepared to give ourselves wholeheartedly to this work of purification. In the mental cleaning and emotional tidying we confront and eventually expel fear, our biggest single obstacle and the enemy of love. This process is ongoing even after we have begun to notice the effects and feel the new joy of freedom. But there is an initial phase when it is new and unfamiliar and we are not yet aware of the results. Then we are most vulnerable to attacks of what the early teachers called *acedia*. This is a complex virus and recurs even when we feel confident we have dealt with it. Discouragement, deflation of energy and hope, a sense of failure and impatience, anger at the people who got us into this business and enviously, unfaithfully, looking over the road at the greener patches of grass: these are the symptoms and like good travellers we have to recognize and endure them. The best cure is to talk about it openly and confidentially with a trusted friend and then to resume the practice as soon as possible. *Acedia* comes in waves, like fog, but between them the view gets better and better and the peace deeper.

Because the work of the first phase is continuous and unfolds at a subtle level it is difficult at times to recognize the benefits. We quickly forget what we used to be like. One of the fruits however, that we can more readily see grow over time is a reduction of the level of fear in ourselves. All sorts of things and situations can breed fear and form crippling patterns that imprison us and reduce our freedom to love. Fear may be aroused by love itself as we feel the terror of being possessed. There is also the fear that we are unlovable, the fear of failure, even of success, rejection, inadequacy, sickness, suffering and death. Essentially fear, not hate, is the contradiction of love; it paralyses love and undermines faith. Even hate or anger against another can mask a disintegrated form of love. No surprise then that the most frequently repeated verse in the Bible is 'do not fear' or that the single commandment of Jesus is 'love each other'.

If fear opposes love, attention cultivates it. In fact the pure attention that is prayer *is* itself a manifestation of love.

55

Christian mystical wisdom says that the work of contemplation is a work of love, not primarily a moral or intellectual work; not a platonic kind of knowledge or an extraterrestrial kind of wisdom; but love. Love is personal, relational; it is embodied in the present. And when it is strong enough, it casts out fear.

Meditatio is the 'pure prayer' described by the early teachers of the tradition. It is pure because it is pure and undivided attention – not thinking about God or solving our problems by thinking but paying attention to God and staring down our anxiety. The reduction of fear levels in our life is one of the more immediately recognizable results of regular practice.

*

Fear is frightened even of itself. We become more insecure and unnatural as soon as we see that we are fearful, especially, when rationally we can see there's nothing to be scared about. But the more we feel frightened of rejection, of the uncertainty of life, of risks, of being known, of giving ourselves, of expressing ourselves, we can see that we are losing our freedom. We become frightened of being afraid and avoid situations where it may be awakened. Fear goes underground and controls us from the unconscious.

In George Orwell's *1984,* Winston, the hero of the book is subjected to a process of brainwashing. Part of his ordeal is the torture in Room 101. What is in the room is not an objective terror; it's purely and terribly subjective. It is what *I* fear most. Whether you have ever seen it before whatever it is you fear will find you there.

The power of fear and the need to expunge it is reflected in the great myths where the hero, on his quest for his origin or for the Holy Grail, has to enter a place of fear. There he finds and slays a terrifying monster which is the embodied object of his fear. Theseus goes into the labyrinth to find the Minotaur; the Anglo-Saxon hero, Beowulf, has to do battle with the monster, Grendal's mother. Jesus, like all of us, sweats fear as he looks at his impending death. These tales and myths speak to us, educate us, because they evoke the Room 101 in us all. In the gospel, where myth is historically enacted, Jesus is a real person who embodies the truths of myth in real time. So must we all. He also seeks and defeats the greatest enemy of all, the one we fear most, and the fear of which we repress most fully: loneliness and death.

*

In this first stage of faith, we plunge deeper than feels comfortable. Sometimes it takes us into a 'thick darkness' where we see nothing and understand less. Sometimes it becomes a 'dark night' where we feel an actual stripping and reduction of our fundamental sense of self. The sickening feeling when we realize that we have irrecoverably deleted an important file from a computer illustrates what we feel like at times in this first phase. Obviously this is not constant. If it were there would be even fewer meditators. But it may recur periodically. Over time we glimpse that the journey of faith is actually being guided by a hand or presence that is not directly perceptible. When we look at where it seems to be it disappears. We're being pushed this way and that into double binds or dead ends. We come to corners where we don't know which way to turn but something from the very depths of our ignorance instructs us. We lean in a direction which turns out to be right though we would never have guessed it. We find ourselves in critical situations we would run a thousand miles from but which we reluctantly see exactly what we need in order to develop.

Never completely lost, there is a subtle sense of guidance, not abstract but intimate, a force to which we give the name 'Holy Spirit'. But there are times when we go into the dark and have to grope our way. We don't see why we are there or where we are going. We don't see the point of anything. It's very hard then even to see why we should keep up the faithful discipline of meditation let alone believe anything. What are we getting out of it except more dense darkness. We don't understand the meaning of the journey or if it a journey at all and not a series of random events only connected in our desperate imagination. Like the desert fathers and spiritual teachers in all traditions who teach faith in such times of hopelessness the Canadian novelist, Margaret Atwood, believes that: 'The well of inspiration is a hole that leads downwards.'

If the hole is there then we have to go into it to discover that it is a depth dimension in which inspiration shines in the dark. The words of the wise and the wisdom of scripture are precious resources and sustenance in making meaning of our experience at these testing times. John Main again:

> The essence of all poverty consists in the risk of annihilation. This is the leap of faith from ourselves to the Other. This is the risk involved in all loving. (*Word into Silence*, p. 21)

5

Stages of Faith: Illumination

New Harmony, Indiana was founded as a new model of society in the early nineteenth century. The Welsh Utopian, Robert Owen, moved there and attempted to build a form of life that would embody his idealistic vision of human nature and its potential. Within a short time the project, like the communes of the sixties, ran headlong into the wall of reality. Owen returned disillusioned to the old world and the town survived sleepily, becoming the centre of the great United States surveying project later in the century until it fell asleep again. It was shaken awake by the new kind of idealism of the Texas oil heiress, Jane Blaffer Owen. Backing up her ideas with faithful investment the town was renovated house by house and became a centre for a visionary kind of spiritual and artistic ecumenism.

In 1991, the year after the closing of the priory, we held the John Main Seminar in New Harmony because Jane who had been inspired by her reading of John Main offered to help subsidize it. Bede Griffiths, the English Benedictine monk who had spent most of his life in India and was revered as one of the great spiritual teachers of the renewal of Christianity was to lead the Seminar. He was insistent that it would focus on John Main's vision of community in the light of meditation. For Fr Bede, John Main was the most important spiritual teacher of the time precisely because how he had helped restore a contemplative practice to ordinary Christian life.

FIRST SIGHT

Several times a day the participants he had drawn from around the world sat with him within the great 'roofless church' that Jane Owen had had built. It was not yet so clear but soon we saw that a great monastery without walls was also being designed there. In his measured English tone and lucid prose Fr Bede, then 85 and just 2 years from his death, spoke twice a day. Walking barefoot, as he preferred, in his ochre sannyasi robes from place to place around the town, he came to exemplify a new idealism uniting ancient wisdom, crossing cultures and serving a forward-looking modernity. Drawing on his own experience in India and John Main's vision as it had transpired so far, he sketched an exhilarating renewed kind of lay monasticism and, by extension, a new kind of church. In between the talks and meditation periods we met to discuss the future of Fr John's project which seemed to have stalled and collapsed but which in fact nobody felt actually had.

It was in those intense, hopeful and often funny discussions that this new utopianism found expression in an organization with a constitution, a chairperson and board. The problem of naming this new being took a long time to resolve. Opinions were divided. Generally people thought it should be descriptive, so it came down to a choice The World Community of Christian Meditation or The World Community for Christian Meditation. We took it to our wise man to decide and he immediately opted for the 'for'. Out of a death a new life had been born with a clear intent and mission – to teach meditation in this tradition in 'a spirit of serving the unity of all'. As we left to implement it we began to see what we had been part of. The wind of a contemplative Pentecost had swept through us and from some-where hard to describe a force had pushed us all back into the real world to speak about silence and to travel far and wide in the cause of stillness.

STAGES OF FAITH: ILLUMINATION

The light shines in the darkness and the darkness cannot over-whelm it. The next phase of faith we will look at now is the illuminative stage. Here are three short sayings of John Main to help us look at the light:

> The risen Jesus can only be seen with the eyes of faith.
>
> We need this clarified vision so that we can see Christ and all life with this new dimension of faith.
>
> To see, to be able to enter this new vision of life, we need the wisdom to penetrate beyond appearances.

So we can now also think of faith as the ability to see the difference between surface and depth, to discern between the transient and what lasts.

*

Meditation reunites the pure beam of light which is fragmented in our perception by the prism of the ego. It leads to a new way of seeing, a way of perception that merges the daily practice of meditation with daily life and work as an integrated way of faith. When we see something, as a child, for the first time we are amazed. The world is teeming with undiscovered wonders and we cannot understand why our elders seem so unimpressed by them. I was waiting once for my bags to appear on the carousel at an airport terminal. It seemed an interminable wait and I just wanted to get out into the fresh air after hours of breathing in artificial environments. Then I noticed a small boy staring at the carousel with transfigured attention. When the light flashed and the bell rang to announce the bags were finally arriving his excitement escalated. When his own bags appeared he shouted the news to his father with an unbearable joy and wonder. I was just pleased my bags had not got lost again. Whoever loved that loved not at first sight? Whoever did not see the world for the first time and fall in love with it? But we gradually forget this first-sight thrill as life becomes routine and stress filters out the joy and wonder. But the first sight experience is recoverable at another level of perception. In fact if it is not recovered we fail to develop. Faith is the capacity to see again for the first time.

*

As life 'comes together' internally and externally, we feel less stressed, more in tune with reality firsthand. Sustaining this process of seeing in faith illustrates why John Main makes a crucial distinction between spiritual practice as a technique and as a discipline.

A technique is something external to us, a tool in our control with which we get desired results by acquiring a useful skill. Of course, it is important to master certain techniques in this way – whether it is learning a foreign language, running a large company or driving a bulldozer. The ego – hopefully in a balanced way –steers the technique and monitors performance results. The difference between a technique and a discipline lies essentially in the attitude that determines our approach to the practice. A discipline (from the Latin *discere*, to learn) runs on faith rather than the will-power needed to master techniques even though there is touch of faith in willpower and of will-power in faith. Discipline however takes the longer and deeper perspective on results. It learns detachment from immediacy and controls impatience and therefore becomes increasingly free from the ego system of control with its complex blend of fear and desire. Eventually discipline transcends egotism and becomes selfless and so more deeply and permanently transformative.

We cannot love or serve others seriously without discipline. We cannot be free without learning discipline. A spiritual practice followed as a discipline raises consciousness beyond the ego level of perception and awakens a new way of seeing. It helps us to see the fruits of the practice in a new way and this gives access to a level of energy beyond what even the biggest or best-directed ego can imagine. It is the non-coercive power of the spirit which the ego's desire for control and domination can never achieve.

Those seeking power through techniques of control will never be at peace. The more power they acquire the more fearful they will become. They may sacrifice health, family and personal integrity in order to succeed but they are unable to make the sacrifice that would truly fulfil their desire by transforming it: the renunciation of the ego. In the discipline of meditation, we make this sacrifice by turning the searchlight of consciousness off ourselves. At first we feel this as loss but later as gain.

In transitioning between the first and the second stages of faith there can be a painful experience of separation or of loss. Changing the direction in which the searchlight of the mind is pointing seems like an extinction of consciousness rather than a liberation. John of the Cross describes this period as the 'night of the senses' in which you move from a familiar devotional kind of religious experience with a significant degree of ego satisfaction into the self-less vision of contemplation. In this phase the feeling of loss affects not only the former, comforting experience of God that a more technique-oriented spirituality gave but faith itself.

Loss is separation. With an unexpectedly hard realism Jesus speaks of his having come to bring not peace but the sword. The sword is not violence but the separation necessary for individuation, the loss that precedes discovery. He teaches radical detachment – poverty of spirit – and warns about the losses and separations necessary to grow into wholeness.

This truth imbues the symbolic breaking of the bread that precedes the time of communion. There is no re-union without the fraction. Separation and loss are naturally repellent because they are painful but the vision of faith allows us to endure them with hope. This hope is born and reborn in the faith experience of discipleship.

*

By learning to be a disciple we discover how to remain faithful and avoid the temptation to run away before the work is completed. Discipleship strengthens us to stand our ground and to persevere. It is rooted in the law of separation and union as lived with particular intimacy in the relationship with the teacher. In its fullest form this relationship realizes the whole process of human development. Between teacher and disciple the bond of faith and love, detachment and union, immanence and transcendence is lived out in daily experience that leads each to a higher level of integration. On his part the disciple's faith needs to be built on total honesty and openness. To play his part the teacher has to be filled with emptiness. He has to be equally committed and detached and to remain faithful even when he is betrayed or rejected.

A teacher embodies loving detachment by remaining in the vortex of paradox, staying both committed and non-possessive, compassionate and non-controlling. Such a teacher merits our faith. Only such a teacher can receive the gift of self which the disciple is learning by imitation and inspiration to make. In the relationship with the teacher the disciple lets go of the entire ego-system of fear and desire. He takes the searchlight of consciousness off himself by pointing it towards the teacher and eventually beyond the teacher to what the teacher himself is turned towards. Few teachers can play this role. Where can we find a teacher of that quality of faith?

Better to let the teacher find you. 'You did not choose me,' Jesus said to his disciples, 'I chose you.' This affronts our ego because we like to be in charge of our own choices. But finding a spiritual teacher is not like signing up for a course at college. The Christian disciple feels he or she has been chosen and has given their consent to this calling. Given the uncool image of Christianity today this may feel like a mixed blessing and many Christians keep their faith in Jesus prudently concealed from those in their social or work spheres who might ridicule it. But Jesus is their teacher nonetheless even if, like

Nicodemus, the disciple goes to him under cover of darkness, fearful of the judgement of others. 'You have one teacher, the Christ', Jesus says, suggesting that the fidelity in the discipleship relationship is mirrored in marriage or other ways of giving self.

Any one else whom the Christian calls 'teacher' does not rival this relationship but reflects it. In this respect Christian discipleship is unlike the *guru* system of the East. The defining distinction of Christian faith is that we find the *sadguru*, the root teacher, in Jesus. By putting his faith in the teacher the disciple learns what it means to let go even when we don't know what comes next. Yet the disciple can enter into this 'darkness of faith' precisely because he has nothing to hold on to. Even the teacher cannot be clung to. In crisis we may feel the grip of his hand but then find he has let go and we are on our own again. But this solitude is paradoxically the condition of the relationship.

'Do not cling to me,' Jesus says to Mary Magdalene. In all the Resurrection appearances, whenever he appears he also quickly disappears again. When he disappears from their sight, however, his disciples do not feel abandoned or afraid; they don't run after him or call him back. It is as if they will never feel bereft again about anything, so unaffected do they seem by his disappearance. A new way of seeing has begun and if once we knew him after the manner of the flesh, we know him thus no longer. The nature of discipleship with Jesus is relationship with *his* emptiness. This is the essence of Christian faith.

Yet, there *is* a personal bond. Jesus tells us to take his yoke, his light yoke, upon ourselves and to follow him without turning back. Discipleship is thus the first wave of the transcendence of the ego. True disciples are as rare as true teachers, however, because it is so easy to get stuck at an early stage of our growth in faith. The price to pay for completing the journey is high. What the East calls the 'grace of the guru' reflects what Dietrich Bonhoeffer called the 'costly grace' of Christian faith. Bonhoeffer said that in responding to the call to follow Jesus, we are not professing a belief but making a pure act of obedience, an act of faith. We do not know where it will lead. All we know for sure is that it will be a way of joy.

*

Discipleship is the transition to the next stage of faith – illumination, enlightenment. As we know this means seeing things and ourselves in a new and clearer perception, without the distortions of the ego and its projections, without the illusions that crystallize from attachments, but like a child seeing everything for the first time as it really is. Gradually both the inner and external dimensions of reality accord with this change of perception. We see this happen as we see the changes in our life that follow upon any sustained act of faith. Values and desires undergo a radical shift. The meaning of work and the sense of what needs to be achieved change. Perception changes the way we live. As William Blake says, 'The fool does not see the same tree as a wise person does.'

This is what is involved in the renaming experience described in the book of Revelation. 'Those who prove victorious' are those who move to the next stage of faith. They will be given a 'secret manna', an interior source of fulfilment sustaining them for the next phase of their journey. They also receive a white stone upon which 'a new name is written known only to the person who receives it'.

What might this enigmatic image mean? If the new name is known only to the person who receives it, then who wrote it? It must also be known at least to the person who wrote it unless they forgot it immediately after writing it. Perhaps there is a way here to understand what is happening in the stage of illumination when we come to a clearer self-knowledge and self-recognition

Naming is an important part of life. Naming a new child or a book, the work we are doing, naming the fear or the emotion affecting us are all important decisions. But this text points to a different kind of naming. It's an unusual naming because the name and the thing named are one and the same. This is the aspiration of language to equate the word with what it designates.

On one occasion Jesus asked his disciples, 'Who do you say I am?' Earlier he had asked 'who do the people say I am' and that hooked their attention. But this new question inviting a personal response is a knockout blow in the process of faith. It is both a powerful moment in the gospel story and in the personal journey of Christian faith because the teacher seems to be putting himself into his disciples' hands by allowing them to name him. He is not looking for their approval. He is not hungry for attention. But he is clearly up to something. By ignoring what they say the people say about him he separates himself from the labels of opinion. After the disciples respond personally he does not comment except to tell them to keep silence and then gives his teaching on the need for the loss of self. He withdraws into an intimate anonymity. At the same moment that he puts himself forward he withdraws into his own emptiness. We are invited to explore his emptiness and to see it is not less than the formless, nameless mystery of the Spirit, the self.

Illumination or enlightenment is a silent, anonymous self-naming. If the name is known only to the person who receives it, it is because it is uttered by the same person. But the act of utterance is made from a new way of seeing. Self-naming is not an act of choice as when we name a child; it's a non-dual process. This self-naming is an awakening in self-knowledge which is a direct expression of faith and inseparable from our knowledge of God and God's knowledge of us. Because we can never know God as an object but only by sharing in the divine self-knowledge of the Spirit, we can know ourselves only because we are known. Our naming *is* this realization. The white stone is seeing things again for the first time.

The deeper we go into faith the more we enter into non-duality, into the oneness that allows for difference without division, for being with without rivalry. 'The love I speak of is not our love for God,' St John says, 'but God's love for us because God loved us first.' Or, St Paul, 'Now we see only reflections in the mirror, mere riddles, but then we shall be seeing face to face. Now I can only know imperfectly, but then I shall know just as fully as I'm known.'

*

A beautiful commentary on this need to be known in order to know is portrayed in Ingmar Bergman's film *Through a Glass Darkly*. It is about a sad dysfunctional family suffering from a chronic lack of communication. There is love but no transmission. The father is a self-obsessed writer who tries to love but has had no real relationship with his children – an emotional lacuna of neglect that shows in the broken personalities of both his son and daughter children and in his mentally ill daughter's marriage. During the film his daughter descends into incurable schizophrenia and is finally taken away at her own request to stay permanently in an institution. The son who is struggling through the loneliness and confusion of adolescence is burdened with guilty and by questions of meaning. At the end of the film he is alone with his father in the early hours of the morning after his sister has been taken away by helicopter. He listens to his father's long monologue about his attempt at faith, his struggle to believe in God. He is speaking from a genuine place and we and his son listen closely to his self-revealing ideas. It is not a ringing endorsement of love, but nor is it without hope. After speaking to his son the father leaves the room to go to bed and it seems that this is the climax, his sincere but failed attempt to express a tenuous faith and to believe what he says. But then the camera turns and focuses on the son. The real climax of the film now occurs in its last line when the son with a new wonder and happiness says simply, 'Papa spoke to me'.

*

The white stone doesn't just drop from the sky onto your head. The name that comes to light is born of a struggle on a journey that takes you into an impenetrable darkness. It is a new birth. Jesus says we are reborn in spirit. It happens in a flash of light but light has to travel a long way before we see it. 'Let there be light' is the beginning of conscious creation, pure consciousness. 'God is light', St John says. Consciousness *is* light and light is a universal symbol of consciousness. In this new light, the Unnameable, the Unknowable, the hundredth name of God, the name that cannot be spoken, that we dare not speak, becomes visible to the eyes of faith.

Our enlightenment and liberation is possible because we are *like* God and the goal of human life is, as the Fathers of the Church insisted, that we become God. Were it not for an intrinsic likeness we would not be able even to conceive this. Someone told me recently that he had been introducing meditation to young children. After he meditated with them one morning, he went on to give them instruction in Christian doctrine. He wanted to speak to them about how we are created in the image of God and he told them the Greek word for image is icon and he said, 'Where do we have icons?' They said, 'On our computer.' He said, 'Right! And what happens when God clicks on our icon?' One child thrust up his hand immediately and said, 'Our heart opens'. Realizing our selves, coming to self-knowledge is the goal of meditation and it is in essence a simple as perhaps is clicking – or double-clicking, for most of us – on the icon of the self.

Faith is the light of consciousness found in the heart. The price of the ticket into the heart is the loss of self. Meditation is the act of faith that leads us on the journey from the head to the heart. It is made as it is *felt*. It is made in the stillness from which action flows. It manifests in deep silence and in truthful speech. We feel it as we meditate because it is a separation preceding union and because every journey is a leaving as well as an arriving. The space between is paradox. Meditation is faith leading to a separation from the familiar world, a comfortably predictable and conventional world. In the daily practice we choose to step outside the ordinary routine for a short time – the TV news, checking email, shopping or managing things. The busyness of the mind planning, imagining, solving problems, wrestling with questions is suspended, just as we suspend our anxieties of the place of departure when we board a plane until we land to meet the problems at the point of arrival.

The teachers of the desert were people of few words. They described this faith journey, the essential nature of prayer, as the 'laying aside of thoughts'. Freedom from thought is not necessarily the same as the total absence of thought but it is the meaning of silence. In the work of silence that we engage with on the 'journey of meditation' the attachments and the compulsions which tie us to the point of departure are gradually undone in the heart. Through the work of a faithful practice they are gradually diluted and eventually evaporate.

You may not know in retrospect the exact point on the flight when you lost your fear; it just slipped away. There may be a phantom of it left but it has lost its power over you. As your heart dilates, fear dilutes. The light of the heart, the light of pure consciousness, the mind of Christ that we find in the heart illuminates everything, pervading our daily mind. Unfortunately it doesn't give readymade answers to all the big questions or solve all daily problems but it gives something for which we become even more grateful, the confidence of faith.

*

Desley was a straight-talking Aussie, a gifted musician, mother of four unique girls. She had suffered greatly when her husband broke faith and left them but she found meditation at the right moment. She was a gifted teacher of meditation with irrepressible energy and enthusiasm. She was one of our best national coordinators until she felt she needed to become more still and she jumped at the opportunity to set up a retreat centre in London. She worked hard on it and enthused all who came in range to help her. Then when we were travelling together to give talks around the country I noticed she was in great pain. Ignoring it she went to visit her mother in Australia and there, collapsed. It was a myeloma. The prognosis was poor and her energy began to bleed away. The physical presence of everything she loved was receding at an accelerated rate. She decided to terminate the chemotherapy when it became too awful and she accepted the next step with grace and humour and was telling her adoring daughters what to do up to her last moment. Shortly before she died I was sitting on the side of her bed as we talked about many things, her suffering and what she had learned through her ordeals but also about the projects on hand she wanted to finish. I asked her if she was curious about what was going to happen next, after the end. She looked thoughtful, looking for the best words, then smiled and said no, she wasn't curious. Then she added, 'I think I know what it is going to be like.' I waited for more and she quietly spoke a few ordinary words which for that short moment became extraordinary windows into reality. Light. Energy. Joy. Love. She was seeing for the first time again and her faith was brilliant.

The answer to the question of Jesus, as to all our big metaphysical questions and the riddles of belief, seems to be just that: not words but the direct illumination of the experience itself. It is a seeing, a first sight knowing, now, *already*, what it's really like.

In that light, the words of John Main about faith may now sound even more directly to the point:

The risen Jesus can only be seen with the eyes of faith.
We need this clarified vision so that we can see Christ and all life with this new dimension of faith.

6

Stages of Faith: Union

As I walked onto the stage with the Dalai Lama for the first session of the Good Heart it suddenly hit me what a razor's edge we were on. I had wanted an interesting life and here it was.

The Dalai Lama had visited our new community in Montreal, 15 years earlier, for midday meditation and lunch. I waited downstairs while he went up to Fr John's room where they spent an hour in private conversation. They emerged with the radiance of new friendship and I sensed that they had communicated within a shared vision of the work for the world that they were each very differently committed to. The Dalai Lama was on the verge of becoming the most popular spiritual figure on the planet as he transformed the pain of his exile and his country's cruel fate into a global compassion and wisdom. Fr John, on a different kind of margin, was helping Christianity evolve by making an ancient Christian wisdom new to his contemporaries and he was also risking a radical innovation in the form of his monastic tradition. Both had the deep solitude of great leadership and I imagined it was in this that they had found their intimacy.

During this visit I was only a young monk in the background for the Dalai Lama. So, when I wrote to the Dalai Lama to ask him to lead the John Main Seminar I was surprised by his prompt and positive response. He remembered the meeting with Fr John very well. I went to see him to discuss the seminar and only realized that we needed a theme when he asked me what I wanted him to speak on. My mind went blank, and then I said, *would he comment on the Gospels. He looked at me curiously and I expected he would refuse but he shrugged his shoulders, said that he didn't know much about them, but he would do his best. I would have to select the passages and give him their context to give him a grip on them and after each of his commentaries we would discuss them. It seemed a great approach until the moment we walked onto the stage. It was then it struck me what a perilous undertaking we had got ourselves into. Although competent members of the community like Clem Sauve from Toronto were managing the event, I suddenly saw what a risk the Dalai Lama had personally taken in accepting. Not all his own supporters felt comfortable with his getting so close to the Christians. I was aware that our community too was risking criticism for putting the sacred texts of our faith into the hands of a 'non-believer'.*

Session by session, meditation by meditation, it dawned on us that the risk was justified. The combination of scripture, sharing and meditation produced a unique intensity and intimacy among all those participating. It was exhilarating, a breakthrough in interfaith dialogue, as it seemed to us, and it initiated many years of friendship and collaboration. Cardinal Basil Hume and my local monastic community warmly supported the Good Heart Seminar. It culminated in an early morning mass at the monastery during which the Dalai Lama commented on the gospel of the day and exchanged the sign of peace with the monks and the Cardinal's representative and later successor, Bishop Vincent Nichols. After breakfast a large gathering of Christian monastics filled the church to hear the Dalai Lama speak about the Rule of St. Benedict. United in our brinkmanship we realized we had not discussed this session. I briefed him on the Rule as best I could in the time available. Then I listened to him incisively take his listeners to its essence, identifying Benedict's vow of 'conversion of life' – the commitment to lived insight into impermanence – as the most Buddhist aspect of Christian monasticism

FIRST SIGHT

Immediately after this final knife edge the Dalai Lama was set to leave. It was over. But until that moment, in all the intensity, I had not realized the end was so imminent. I found myself standing at the door saying my farewell and then realized what a very un-Buddhist and un-Benedictine thing had happened. I had become attached. The object I had become attached to was on the point of separation and a great pain filled me and my eyes filled with tears. He registered this and looked deeply into me and laughed. We embraced and he was gone. I knew again, but differently, what a big emptiness fullness needs.

John Main again, on what is happening when we meditate in Christian faith:

> We pay attention to our own true nature and by becoming fully conscious of the union of our nature with Christ, we become fully ourselves. (*Word into Silence*, p. 18)

Here he describes a relationship between those who have made a reciprocal investment of faith in each other. This illuminates a universal law – operating from the smallest to the greatest of our relationships – which reveals that ultimately reality itself *is* relationship:

> Every personal, loving relationship has its source in the movement from lover to beloved though it has its consummation in a holy, simple communion. (*Word into Silence*, p. 53)

We have been looking at faith with the help of Christian mystical wisdom and its template of the stages by which the journey of faith into full human flourishing unfolds. We have seen the preparatory phase of purification leading to the phase of enlightened seeing. Now we will explore the blossoming of faith which is union. These are not abstract ideas. Human development moving towards its completion and self-transcendence passes through these stages and there is remarkable agreement across the mystical traditions concerning the phases of the process. Of course, along with the universal law there is an individual uniqueness. Psychologically and culturally, the timetable and context will always be particular. It is always the human journey, however, and that is why all wisdom traditions understand each other so well at this spiritual level of the inner journey.

We are more conscious of the stages unfolding if we have a strong contemplative practice. Without meditation the danger is that we sleepwalk through these stages of life sometimes, especially in a culture as self-distracted and anxious as ours, in a semi-comatose state. Then instead of responses made in faith we have knee-jerk reactions to events and crises but no deeper sense of their meaning or pattern. Meditation does not ensure we can predict the future. We don't know where the journey of faith will lead us but it is enough to know it is a journey and we are empowered to remain faithful to it. Achieving self-determined goals is not the issue. Being faithful is. As an old rabbi once said, 'God doesn't expect us to succeed. But we are not allowed to give up.'

We progress by doing the next thing we have to do as well as we can: one day at a time, as the wisdom of the 12-step programme puts it. Often people in recovery will tell you to the exact day, how long it has been since they took a drink or last did drugs. Their experience of the programme by this stage may have become not just a crisis therapy but a deep spirituality. But they never forget it is also time-bound and fragile. It is sobering and strengthens faith to ask: *How long have I been doing this? How long have I been meditating?* The other time-centred question, *how long does it take?* becomes less intrusive as faith deepens. It *is* happening; that is the important thing.

As faith grows, and with it our track record of commitment and experience of transcendence, time itself undergoes a change because the mental construct of past, present and future changes. The idea of time has many expressions, from chronological to biological, emotional to cosmic. We sometimes feel we have lived a lifetime in a moment. We can feel time as a crucifixion or as a resurrection. The vast figures measuring cosmic time in an expanding universe can seem overwhelming but the few years of a human life can seem more significant and precious. Time and mortality live out the drama of birth and death and the painful mystery of separation. In the light of faith we come by stages to see the all-pervading mystery of union.

Changing perspectives on time release the wisdom potential in the ageing process. There is not much else to justify it. But the longer we live the more we see a pattern of losing and finding and sense the something that holds them together. This can give detachment (sometimes at the price of a waning of passion). We grudgingly accept that the fulfilment of desire does not constitute true happiness. This is the wisdom of mortality rather than enlightenment. Nevertheless it allows the present moment to become more real to us and so we can become more conscious even as our powers dwindle. The chronological countdown is now a background awareness, less of a compulsive concern. We are not looking at our watch so often.

That anyway is how it could be. Everyone has to face the same journey and go through the stages but we can do so more or less smoothly and wisely. It's better to go through them gently, acceptingly, throughout life rather than leaving all the learning to pile up for the last stage of life. By then, we may be so preoccupied with medication and comfort levels, struggling with denial of death and the anxiety of the end that we are unaware of the real meaning of what is unfolding. Life is meaningful because it is a transcendent preparation for death. It is awful to imagine being totally unprepared for it after a life in which we did nothing consciously to deepen our faith. Remember the experience of not revising for an exam and undergoing the fear and stress the week before you sit it. The better prepared we are for dying, the more fully we live and the smoother the times of transition. Eastern wisdom speaks here of the law of karma. The doctrine of the catholic tradition would say we make up for lost time and finish the purification process in purgatory. All agree, however, that we are better prepared for the final stage ultimate union if we seriously attend to getting ourselves ready now and pass through the purifying and illuminative stages earlier in the journey. Daily meditation is simply a way of faith that focuses this preparation.

*

This consummation of union, whether it is called nirvana, liberation from rebirth, enlightenment, moksha or heaven is part of the common ground of all religious wisdom when we understand religion in its mystical dimension. It refers to the experience of oneness, the transcendence of the ego's centre of consciousness, the transformation of the dualistic mind, the movement from the mind's self-mirroring complexities into the simplicity and pure vision of the heart, the non-duality of the spirit. With a silent passion deeper than their words and differences, all religions point to this. If they do indeed teach this way and not just pay lip-service to it, religion offers our often sad and battered humanity a reasonable and empowering hope.

We both lose and find ourselves in the otherness of ultimate reality. This is easy to say but it is a hard paradox to wrestle with. It demands a deepening faith commitment. When the master class of life has taught us enough, commitment meets detachment and solitude, the recognition and acceptance of our uniqueness, becomes more attractive and even easier. We gradually withdraw from unnecessary activity and distraction. We become freer from compulsions and addictions. This is a stage that may match our ageing process but some young people experience it too. It challenges us because we find ourselves attracted to less conventional and socially approved values. A husband or wife may find that they want more quiet and less activity and this may create conflict with a partner who may feel hurt and see it as a pulling away from their union, a kind of adultery with God. Faith requires a balancing of commitments. And no one said it would be easy.

But as the third stage of faith begins to dawn, it opens – as faith ever does – to a new horizon in which we both withdraw and return to others in a new way. We learn better to allow the other to be *other* and not allow our projections to distort our love for them. We have to give ourselves to them and learn better to ask nothing in return. Ultimate reality is approached by this process of faith in which the self and the other are newly discovered through the losing and finding. Faith then blossoms as the most comprehensive form of love – agape. The vision it bestows is that ultimate reality is love.

As we come closer to the goal we lose ourselves more completely in the encounter with in paradox. This makes difficult things easier to accept because we sense they are not just contradictions and random sufferings but part of an integrated pattern. For example, an illness which begins with grief, complaint and bitterness may end as a blessing by teaching us a greater understanding of wholeness and well-being. We find ourselves as a simpler person than we thought we were, and recognize the new name we have been given and that is known only to the Self who spoke it in love. Losing and finding, woundedness and healing, living and dying, are the cycles of growth – death and rebirth. As long as we need to, we repeat this cycle with ever deeper experience of faith. What is born will die, and what dies is reborn. Each breath of our respiration cycle teaches us this as does every faithful relationship or commitment in our life. It is both wonderful, revelatory, instructive and tiring. We begin to long for release from the cycle and this release is what Christian faith aspires to in Resurrection.

If Christ is not risen, St Paul said, we have no hope. But if he is, then even now, as we are tossed up and down on the tides of life we can experience something of what resurrection means. We feed, as it were, on the future not as a dream or gamble but as a present reality. Resurrection is what eventually breaks us out of the cycle of death and rebirth. The more we experience it the more we can say:

I live no longer but Christ lives in me.

But who is the *I* that says this extraordinary thing? As long as we talk about it we are not yet fully in it. We cannot know the risen Christ as an object of knowledge. As soon as he is objectified in the dualistic mind he vanishes. In the spirit, though, where non-duality has been transcended, we can see him. Christian faith which is built on this can also build the most beautiful belief systems and temples of worship. But ultimately it is built upon a vanishing experience which keeps us forever children on the way of faith.

Learning to meditate teaches us this firsthand. The novitiate in monastic life also illustrates it. It is a year (now sometimes two) during which the new monk is simplified and gently regressed to a point where he can properly begin his new journey of faith. When you are just setting out on this journey with a monastic teacher you are required to make certain external renunciations and symbolic, rather theatrical, changes in lifestyle. I remember from my novitiate, with John Main as my novice master, how tough and yet exhilarating this can be. My first test was to give up smoking. Fr John made it clear this was necessary. It was not his style to approach it as an imposition but to help you see for yourself. He managed eventually to help me do this after many failed attempts to free myself from the addiction. Smoking, he explained, was incompatible with meditation which had brought me to this life, because it was a negation of freedom and true love of self. Meditation is about freedom and loving one self. The logic was unarguable but it didn't get me there. I had been trying to quit unsuccessfully for 6 months and was quite anxious about going cold turkey on the day of my clothing in the monastic habit. I wanted, as it were, to exchange one habit for another. A visiting young monk who had just taken simple vows consoled me, as he thought, by advising me not to worry too much about it. Just smoke discretely, he hinted, and then after the novitiate, once I had been accepted into the community, no one would object to my smoking openly. It was a wonderful piece of advice because it cleared by mind in an instant. Giving up smoking then became a simple, if not physically easy process. The rest of the novitiate was an exhilarating flight of freedom despite or perhaps because of all the restrictions. I was freely accepting them however irritating or petty they seemed at times. I sunk immediately to the bottom of the social pyramid of the monastery. I had no political significance, my voice was barely listened to and I was expected to live without complaining even when I felt ignored or exploited. I had no money and couldn't go out without permission. It was elementary monastic living made easy but, given the intransigence of my ego as I now discovered it, perseverance would have been impossible without a teacher. When the novitiate ended I was entitled to go to community meetings and I was asked to think about where to do my studies. I had regained a certain social status by taking my vows. Even though the vow was supposed to be a further renunciation of status it was in my novitiate that I was really 'poor' and marginal. With status complexity returned. Only meditation reminded me I was still and would always be a novice.

*

In the early days of learning to meditate the novice can enjoy beginner's luck. Without knowing how we are doing it, we spontaneously find ourselves saying the mantra with complete abandon and poverty of spirit is tasted in its true nature. For a brief spell the ego puts up no resistance to grace

After this, however, the gravitational pull of the ego is reasserted but in ways that brings true union closer. It is like the resistance necessary for a pulley to lift and move a heavy object. Even the isolationist ego then becomes part of the great wave carrying us to our goal. Union is the condition of oneness, the end of isolation and the beginning of love in ever widening circles. It is not a state of mind, always shifting and conditioned by successive events. Union is an irreversible stage of the journey that is achieved more by shedding desires and preconceptions than by setting and achieving targets. We can have ecstatic moments of union but the very concept of ecstasy is spatial. *Ecstasis* means to 'stand outside'. In union, the 'Kingdom' experience, there is neither inside nor outside. 'You cannot say look here it is or there it is.' Union is simple. God, according to Thomas Aquinas, is infinitely simple.

So if talking about it shows that we are not there, why bother to talk about it?

Because it can help and it is better to know that it is there even if we do nothing yet to cooperate with the pull it exerts on us. Of course talking can easily be counter-productive and a substitute for the real thing. If we talk too much about it or for the wrong motives, then it can confuse and mislead. But if it comes from the place of beginning and does not try to describe the goal too fully it can be helpful in deepening faith. The best teachers know that they are not really competent. They ask themselves how they can talk about what they haven't fully experienced yet. Here I am, they say, telling people how to meditate and how important it is for the world while day after day I am battling with my distractions and other problems like an absolute beginner. It's their day-to-day faithfulness, of course, not their perfectionism, that justifies them and makes them effective for others in ways they might never see. The word has to be shared and passed on to the next and hopefully better generation of teachers. Better to have humility and self-doubt than to be the kind of teacher who feels it is their ordained destiny to instruct the world in their wisdom. Of course, whenever we talk about the stage of union or use the word *God* we are to some degree outside it. But being incomplete is not hypocrisy. Speaking about what we barely know is an occasion for the realism that makes it worthwhile to encourage others that faith is worth taking seriously. And that we only have to begin.

Another reason for speaking about it is that if you have had any kind of glimpse or beginner's luck with God, it is simply the most interesting and important thing in the world and in your own experience. It can spoil you for other things life has to offer.

But even if you know how little you know, you know enough to say for certain this is absolutely worth knowing better.

*

In trying to communicate faith we are also deepening it. But the meaning of any communication is in its context. Talking about the spiritual path of life outside a context contemplative practice always seems to me unsatisfactory, incomplete and unserious. That is why I try to ensure that whenever I speak about these things there is a period of meditation included. This helps me too because it feels as if the shortcomings of the talk are compensated by the teaching of the experience itself. Perhaps this was part of John Cassian's thinking too when he said that *Magistra experientia*, experience is the teacher.

Of course the taste of union does not depend on people speaking about it. If we remember our childhood's moments of mystical experiences we see that the vision can come through any medium at any time because it is omni-present. You never know where or when. It is unpredictable and always a surprise even when, like the sunrise, you have been waiting for it a long time. This purely *given* experience of grace may therefore seem random but in fact in its coming it feels, like beauty itself, inevitable, necessary and punctual. But as soon as we begin to conceptualize the experience it is moved to another level of perception. It fades and recedes from the level of first sight. We are left holding a thought or memory and our beliefs cluster around the idea as something distinct from the experience. You may soon be convinced the experience is untrustworthy or even that it is dangerous to try to return to that level of direct knowing and that the belief is safer and easier to stay with.

Inevitably we form some beliefs based on experience. They are not substitutes for the real thing and may even be touched by the grace of the seeing. But as beliefs they remain limited as signs. Provided we haven't lost contact with the poverty of spirit from which the experience arises, the interpretations and beliefs we form will be taken for what they are, pointers along the footpaths of faith. If we return frequently to the place of beginning without demand or expectation for experience we will be saved from the error of confusing faith and belief. We won't be living on the capital of past memories. We won't be thinking, as sometimes happens with artificially induced experiences that flood the weak ego, this belief of mine is a revelation that sets me apart from others.

The sets of beliefs by which we try to express this experience of grace will feel most at home in the paradoxical. The contemplative understanding is often best conveyed in symbols rather than logical definitions. According to the greatest minds that's the nature of all dogma; ideas are fingers pointing at the moon. All creedal statements are true as symbolic statements. Thomas Aquinas, the architect of the *Summa Theologica*, which became the highway code of Catholic theology, overwhelmingly experienced the difference between faith and belief at the end of his life. Even before he stopped writing he knew that anything we say about God is by way of analogy, metaphor and symbol. Like beautiful religious art the best doctrines are meant to inspire first sight not to become cult objects in themselves.

Dogmas held lightly like this, in a non-dogmatical way, help us to live better, more clearly and happily. We need a belief system as we need signposts in our own language on a long journey. They are familiar reminders of the meaning of progress: fidelity to the path, returning continuously to first sight, to the experience in itself and remaining open to the unexpected – an essential aspect of a life lived faithfully. Diversions can be part of the route too. This way of balancing being faithful with holding to beliefs reduces the effects of the extreme individualism and self-reliance in which modern culture conditions us and which brings so much anxiety and sadness. Having no beliefs except those of our own making or patched together from random sources is as unsatisfactory as clinging to beliefs with which we were spoon fed and told never to question. Either extreme blocks grace and alienates us from the simplicity, the union that we long for.

*

Jesus says that a pure heart sees God. Union with God is the vision of God in faith. It seems natural to use vision to describe the ultimate stage of faith. But it has its dangers because we are used to seeing and interpreting objects that we look *at*. This cannot apply to our vision of God. So the great teachers undermine the metaphor of vision even as they use it. Faith they say is a seeing but it is a seeing of things unseen. It is not objectified vision. We see but we do not *look* at. Or as I have quoted before and like to recall often, St Irenaeus in the second century: *We can never see God as an object but only by sharing in God's own self-understanding.*

Because faith is a type of seeing – but not of the *looking at* kind – we are not waiting for images, revelations, extraordinary things to happen during meditation. If these do occur we should move on and leave them behind as quickly as possible. As soon as we look back we risk the fate of Orpheus. He went into the underworld to recover his wife Eurydice and was told to lead her back but not to look back. He did look back and this time lost her forever. If we look too long at our own experiences we risk becoming ensnared in the past and trapped by our own self-fixation. What we look at is not always the same as what we are meant to see. Learning this in meditation has a significant effect on all aspects of our life. It opens a depth dimension and gives us the *more* we are always thirsting for. However attractive or repellent, the surface is the surface, not the whole picture, icebergs are tips of a greater invisible mass. This understanding is born of faith and becomes embedded as a wisdom teaching in our experience. When 'nothing seems to be happening' in our meditation it reminds us not to judge the book by its cover and to trust that something surely is happening precisely because nothing seems to be happening.

Union is 20-20 vision. We come to this perceptual aspect of faith as we come to a faith-training exercise like meditation having been conditioned by those ways of seeing that have become dominant in our culture. Today perception has been heavily influenced by the screen. In an era where virtual reality has been so perfected looking at the real world directly or even reading from a printed page are fading or specialized ways of perception. Students find libraries oppressively quiet and prefer to do their research in the dining halls on their laptops. Nature programmes makes us gasp at the close-ups of the wildlife that is in the garden a few metres away.

Some cultural historians think this vast change in ways of seeing began about the twelfth century. Until then the page of the book or manuscript was not something you looked *at* as if it were a screen made of paper or parchment but it was something you moved *through*. We still speak of being 'drawn into' or 'absorbed' by a good book. One source for the word *page* suggests vines fastened by a stake and formed into trellises. This image leads to the columns of writing on a scroll. The 'written page' was not divided up into paragraphs until relatively recently and did not even have spaces between words. So, the reader had to move through it and make sense of it by reading aloud. Thus the word became flesh on your lips. After the twelfth century the page started to become a form of communication closer to our screen as something silently looked at. The audible murmur of reading yielded to a more individual experience. Later there came indexes written at the back of the book and footnotes and so on, cross-referenced pages in a whole work that could not all be seen at once.

*

Faith is not an objective, looking-at kind of experience. The visual metaphors used to illustrate it ('Oh, I see what you mean!') need to be complemented by auditory symbols ('Yes, I am hearing what you say'). Faith may in fact be even better understood as a listening to the *logos*, which means not a single spoken or text message from God but the inherent rationality and coherence in all things at every level of experience. The *logos* is in everything or there would be nothing. Even the absurd or the random merely hides the *logos* from a surface perception but with the eyes and ears of wisdom even these experiences reveal meaning. The *logos* is as ancient a concept in Western thought as the *tao* or the *dharma* is in Eastern philosophy. In Christianity, more influenced at first by Greek and Semitic than by Asian thinking, the *logos* was the Word of God, the self-pronunciation and self-naming of the divine. It ripples through the cosmos ('order') as we today imagine the background radiation of the Big Bang diffused everywhere. In the human who is a microcosm of all the worlds the logos is self-aware. Whether through seeing or hearing, union is achieved through faith that merges deep vision and attentive listening.

> What we shall be has not yet been disclosed but we know that when it is disclosed we shall be like him because we shall see him as he is. (1 Jn. 3:2)
>
> The words I have spoken to you are spirit and they are life. (Jn. 6:63

First sight is seeing what is. Deep listening is an act of radical obedience to what is. Obedience means more than just doing what you're told. It is becoming the truth you hear. The Latin *obaudire* links listening to obedience. St Benedict speaks of obedience without delay as the means of uniting the mind of the disciple with that of the master. St Augustine brings these two forms of perception together when he speaks about the spiritual senses or the 'inner sense' and by saying that hearing is a degree of vision.

The 'kingdom of heaven' or the 'reign of God' are the gospel terms for union with God and others in the fully developed form of love without boundaries called 'agape'. Jesus speaks simply about these realities but he says you can't say 'look, here it is or there it is' because it is non-spatial and non-dual; it is, in fact, both in you *and* among you. This non-duality does not exclude it from day to day reality, from 'ordinary' sense perception or rational observation. The non-dual contains the dual. Reason can operate in the spiritual realm. The point is that union is not limited by any form of perception. The Kingdom is here and now but also super-spatial and transtemporal. As with the spirit you can't say where it comes from or where it is going but it's always present. It's this assurance that allows us to get on with the work we have to do while following the way of faith with complete commitment. Raising a family, meditating alone, developing one's gifts, going through grief or celebrating success: none of these states need interrupt the way of faith. To evoke the ordinariness of this mystery of reality Jesus uses parables about natural growth, family relationships, finding and losing things or helping the helpless to describe the process of faith that awakens the kingdom. As he presents it heaven is a present reality or an eternal process rather than a place or a reward. Union, once it is uncovered, is boundless.

Coming into union means we have never arrived at a final destination because the journey has become limitless. 'To seek God is to find God,' says Gregory of Nyssa but equally, he says, 'to find God is to seek God'. We set out endlessly on a penetration of reality moving towards an ever-receding horizon. Peace means the acceptance of this freedom from limitation. Modern cosmology observes us inhabiting an expanding universe and offers us a new metaphor the earlier masters would have enjoyed. We are also told however that it is space not matter that is expanding. We are being infinitely stretched into nothingness by what we inhabit and because what inhabits us is expanding endlessly. It is what we call and strive for as freedom.

*

Growing in faith throws opens the doors of perception and frees us from the limits of the dualistic mind. But we remain (or even better) capable of catching trains on time, questioning bills when we have been overcharged and learning how to create a blog. But we also become more simple, more childlike. The most obvious quality of childhood that separates it so vastly from the adult world is the child's lack of self-consciousness. Adolescence ends tour time in Eden, but we never completely forget it or stop feeling some nostalgia for it. Children often amaze us by what seems their preternatural wisdom but in fact it is quite natural. They are so close to the source. Our learning to meditate reminds us that their capacity for wisdom and insight is still within us if we too can become 'like little children' – which is different from acting childishly. Children lack information and experience – a lack which makes them vulnerable – but their natural insight and wisdom can make the elders look foolish.

Inevitably the Garden of Eden is put behind us one day. After tasting the apple of knowledge Adam and Eve saw for the first time that they were naked and hid from God.

> Adam replied, 'I heard the sound of you in the garden and I was afraid because I was naked, so I hid.' God said, 'who told you that you were naked?' (Gn 3:10)

As always the questions of God lead us to self-knowledge. Finding ourselves east of Eden, realizing what fear and duality means and that we are divided and afraid, suffering from shame and self-consciousness, are what we call the 'fall' and it is a necessary stage in human development. Despite all our infantile attempts at regression which we call entertainment, despite DisneyWorld and videogames for the ungrownup, there is no going back. Union is not re-found in the *uroboric* state of the past, symbolized by the self-sufficient serpent eating its own tail, when we lived in a self-secure world. It lies in the future, the union of the deep present, that we realize by awakening to who and where we are now. We are impelled to become childlike but we can't go backwards. First we must confront our painful state of exclusion and separation in a world of disappointed dreams and false desires. When we first sit to meditate at the outset of this journey of faith we find ourselves awkwardly self-conscious, individualistic, disconnected, lonely and also embarrassingly bad at concentrating. But this initial awakening is a great leap forward. We make it best by being still together within the community of love that begins to replace the sense of exclusion and that will help us to keep growing in faith. Without community the way of faith is almost impossible. It is so easy to become self-delusional. One of the flaws of modern culture is that there are so few people who understand what community of this kind really means.

*

We begin. We persevere. We start again. And there is always another stage, another peak. Gradually and imperfectly we approach what we dare to call maturity. We struggle with self-consciousness in order to become fully conscious and, with individuation in order to belong. So we find ourselves in a form of community which we had not imagined could have existed. It is a community arising from the experience of communion born in silence. Unlike other interest groups or friendships based primarily on what attracts us to each other a community of faith becomes a community of love formed by forces that move us to change without the use of force or rivalry. We learn to make relationships at a spiritual level; we learn to handle loss and suffering and to celebrate expansion at the same level. This forming of spiritual consciousness does not alienate us from the world of day-to-day responsibilities but makes us handle ourselves better in this realm. But then, just as we see that we are managed better in life, we feel called to another stage, a deeper degree of union.

Now the challenge is to transcend self-consciousness, the ego itself. In the irrepressible process of human development there is always a call to go deeper. It is what we call growing up and explains why even in middle or old age and the young look on the elders as ancient beings who have seen it all and been exhausted by it, the conscious human being will privately feel he or she has still a long way to go before being complete. In the deeper stages of union we find ourselves letting go of self-consciousness and acting as if the 'right hand doesn't know what the left hand is doing'.

> The monk who knows that he is praying is not truly praying. The monk who does not know that he is praying is truly praying. (Evagrius, Chapters on Prayer)
>
> The life I now live is not my life but the life that Christ lives in me. (Gal. 2:20)

Mindfulness might be confused on occasions with mindlessness. The illuminative stage begins to burn away the self-consciousness of the dualistic mind as the sun burns away a morning mist. Union is the consummation of faith. But in the turbulence of the purification process stage or even in the lightning flashes of illumination we still do not fully grasp what union means or what it costs.

Union develops without our realizing it. Aquinas says that it is like seizing and being seized at the same time. The Sufi poets use the erotic language of paradox, losing self at the moment of self-discovery. The soul devours and is herself devoured, embraces and is unexpectedly embraced. It seems hard to describe this level of union without sexual metaphors and many of the mystics, from the poet of the *Song of Songs*, to Rumi and St John of the Cross, use erotic imagery to describe the most spiritual stage of faith – union with God. This is evocative but also odd because of all human passions, sex is most painfully connected to infidelity.

In pre-modern societies and in the major religions sex has been understood as a sacred energy. It is only in a consumer society, built upon the escalation of desire, not its transformation, that sex becomes a way of selling things and the test of 'serious' relationships. However much sex in real life, outside the fantasy realm, is limited by physical and psychological constraints it is still an energy of union with the divine that flows from and back to God between ourselves and the material world. God as the best theologians recognize has an erotic side to him. To repress this energy or to become obsessed with it is to be equally unfaithful to this sacred force. Sex is a major instrument in the spiritual repertoire by which we taste union in sacramental moments. But it cannot be isolated and enjoyed outside the context of faith for long without damage. There are also other levers by which we are lifted out of the ego-centric orbit.

Sometimes the means of transcendence are not as pleasurable as sex. I was once riding a bicycle in heavy London traffic and was knocked off my bike by a careless turn by a van-driver. In an instant I was aware I was no longer negotiating the cars and trucks but lying in the middle of the road seeing the world from ground level and quite probably facing an early retirement. Wheels whirled round me mercifully avoiding me. Time had stopped or slowed down dramatically. I felt precarious but wonderfully free and contented – for how long it didn't matter. I was aware of the danger and still unaware of my broken finger but the peace and sense of oneness free of all fear or anxiety were complete. I could have rolled over and gone to sleep but I didn't need to sleep because I felt totally awake and relaxed. Then suddenly I was aware of someone standing over me and obviously very anxious and afraid. The driver responsible for this interesting experience bent over me and asked if I was alright. I felt, but without resentment, that he might be less concerned about how I was than about the police. I didn't deny him some altruistic compassion but self-concern was mixed with it. So it seemed to me quiet objectively at the time. It didn't concern me and if that was forgiveness then it was a quite natural forgiveness.

Such moments, in and out of time, happen: moments of aesthetic delight, of mishaps, moments of love and rapture, intellectual insight, contact with music, flashes in the mundane that permit us to see what lies below the surface. In these moments we perceive who and where we truly are, how our social identity is not the true self. When we see the un-nameableness of reality like this, it's so simple, so obvious; it's just here where we are.

The goal of life, however, is not to multiply these flashes of illumination revealing union but to leave the light on, to live in faith, to expand in love. We don't meditate as a way of faith each day to increase the frequency of mystical experiences. If that was what we wanted we might as well take something intravenously. We meditate to grow in faith.

*

Faith is active in love. We meditate to arrive at continuous prayer where we remain at home in the place of union while keeping our feet on the ground. The 'further shore' is not a distant goal but a simple unification of all worlds. So, when we get knocked off the road, we know quickly what has happened and get back up on the bike. Learning how to integrate this dimension of reality with ordinary life and work is the art of living in faith. It is hard to learn alone especially at first. If we are lucky we have the grace of knowing someone, they are hard to find, in whom union is unbroken, integrated and dynamic.

For me that was perceptible in John Main. To learn from him wasn't just a matter of hearing him speak. It was living with him, seeing how he lived, hearing how he dealt with difficult people, including me. It was not only *what* he said but who he was, consistently, in many different situations each day. Theory – what I have called a belief system – has much to give for the journey. It would be harder without it. But it is at this personal level that the greatest teaching is given and that most is learned. Here too is found the conviction that lies deeper than the mind, that the ultimate reassurance happens. In starting any work – a career, a relationship, meditation – we need a wise blend of affirmation and correction. Someone to say well done and also not so well done. We need to be reassured that we are learning and we can keep going. Despite our faults, we have the potential to go the whole course.

To know someone in whom union has happened and continues to unfold at new depths while you know them is a great grace. It means we sense what we too might be capable of. Imitation through inspiration is an integral part of teaching. The teacher is not just a hero we admire and put on a pedestal. A hero is somebody who makes us feel a little inferior: 'wow! I could never do that. I can never run a 3.43-minute mile; I couldn't climb Everest, become a brain surgeon or learn Spanish'. A teacher shows you what you *can* do and empowers you to do it, helping as much as is necessary but not taking away your privilege of making mistakes. Teaching is service not manipulation or substitution. It is the motivation for teaching meditation. It is at the deepest level the meaning of Jesus too.

We learn from good teachers how to be faithful. When we see in them how faith flowers in union we hold our beliefs more wisely and lightly. Doubt and insecurity may recur from time to time but with less power to upset us. Doubt and fear even serve to strengthen our faith rather than to disrupt it. The conviction and certainty of faith this process leads to does not deter all emotional or intellectual attacks though it can weather all storms. In the end there is boundless oneness in love but until the end we can't be absolutely certain of anything. Maybe everything that we feel about the progression of faith and the stages of human development is true. But who knows? Maybe, too, the light just goes out. That's the end: one big anaesthesia. Without that wiggle room for doubt faith could not deepen.

But logically, if the *logos* is the coherence of things and if the world has meaning, then there is a continuation of this process beyond all horizons. It is conceivable that it is logical up to the very last minute and then it becomes illogical because something completely unimaginable happens. Perhaps there is nothing except meaningless expansion of space without *my* being in any way part of it. Yet as we grow in faith this seems less and less likely just as it's unlikely that the sun won't rise tomorrow or set tonight. The reason is in how faith reveals love.

So in the end it does seem that the goal of faith is communion. Then the prayer of Jesus for all humanity makes sense: 'May they be one as we are one. As You, Father are in me and I in you, may they be in us.'

Every personal, loving relationship has its source in the movement from lover to beloved though it has its consummation in a holy, simple communion. (*Word into Silence*, p. 53)

7

Christian Faith

Monte Oliveto. For 20 years we have had an international silent meditation retreat here where sensual beauty and spiritual energy combine. Bernardo Tolomei, the founder of the Monastery of Monte Oliveto Maggiore, the motherhouse of the Benedictine Olivetan Congregation, was born in Siena, a city of saints, in 1272. His noble family were the Pope's bankers. He was a brilliant lawyer and joined a confraternity, part of the great devotional movements that swept Italy at his time. Suffering from damaged eyesight, a canonical impediment to ordination, he decided to withdraw from the world and settled with two companions in a remote part of his estates, the crete senesi on which the monastery dramatically rests today. They lived in the spirit of the desert monks which led inevitably to the development of a community. Bernardo integrated it into the church by adopting the Rule of St Benedict.

It is difficult not to be moved by St Bernardo Tolomei. He avoided power even in the monastic world he created. For many years he declined to be abbot of the monastery he founded. Born to privilege he freed himself by his faith from the prison of wealth and hierarchy. In 1348 the plague that devastated all of Europe, reducing the population by two-thirds, arrived in Siena. With some of his monks Bernardo left his safe monastery to return to the city to care for the sick and dying. He caught the plague and died with them. His body disappeared into a common grave, hermit, monk in community and active servant of the poor.

His successor, my present abbot, is in charge both of the monastery and the whole congregation of 23 houses. He has always supported my work in teaching and travelling in the monastery without walls. About to retire, he asked me to speak about our meditation oblate community at the General Chapter, held every 4 years to review the life of the congregation and elect the abbot general. Over the years the monks had formed a generally positive view of what I was doing and accepted the peculiarities of my life with its many exceptions to the Rule. I missed the common life and always felt at home when I returned there. I had also often wished the meditation could have had more influence on the monastic institution but had learned to let go of these expectations.

I spoke as invited and there was time for questions. To everyone's mild surprise one monk launched into a detailed but rather confused refutation of meditation. The points he made were familiar enough to me, although they are made much less frequently today since the teaching and the community has become more part of the Christian mainstream. As he spoke I felt an initial disappointment then a recognition of the moment and a profound gratitude for what was happening. In the next 2 hours an unscheduled discussion on meditation and the way of faith it represented received a positive affirmation from the most intellectual and spiritual of my brother monks. The monk who had caused this graciously apologized the next day for his tone and we sat next to each other in a friendly way during the following meetings. It had meant more to me perhaps than the others, this moment of affirmation and acceptance.

As the meditation community enters a new phase of its journey, it felt good to hear this explicit support one after another from my monastic brethren. But now – in our Meditatio program – we are making a new leap of faith reaching out beyond the spiritual comfort zone to dialogue with the secular world. As we explore the meaning of meditation for children, mental health, business and finance, the environment and social justice, the meaning of faith itself is being put to a new test.

We have looked at three stages of the inner journey of human development in the light of faith. These stages are universally recognized and apply to every human being regardless of faith or culture. We also eat and digest, breathe and move in essentially the same way as members of the same species. Spiritually we run on the same operating system.

But the differences are as important as the similarities. Perhaps there would be no recognizable similarities without the differences. Faith is human; it is the capacity of the human being for transcendence and love. It is not limited to a particular religion or even to religious people as such. The atheist or agnostic also lives by faith in the sense I am suggesting. Faith is like meditation which is also universal and a way of developing our faith to its fullest capacity. We find meditation in all traditions as part of the human heritage. Yet we can speak without contradicting the universality about Christian meditation or Buddhist meditation. So too, there is also Christian faith.

I would like now to explore what faith means in the context of Christian identity. We have seen how faith is more than belief. It forms but transcends belief-systems. It is about personal self-giving in a commitment of trust, perseverance, self-transcendence. It opens to spiritual vision. It is the matrix of love. St Irenaeus, as we have seen, said the beginning is faith, the end is love; and the union of the two is God. Faith is active in love.

Christian faith has differences compared with other expressions of faith but it is not competitive with them. Religions are the conduits for their unique expression of faith. What is confident of its uniqueness does not need to compete with other unique expressions. Competition and intolerance are more likely to creep in when the contemplative dimension has slipped out of the mainstream of a religion and the belief system has assumed a disproportionate importance. Competition corrupts religion and renewal begins by returning to the founder's vision and the contemplative experience. The great spiritual teachers of humanity did not compete.

*

John Main will again help us to begin:

> We are reluctant to admit that we are the sick and sinful whom Jesus came to heal. We prefer our self-protecting isolation to the risk of the face-to-face encounter with the Other in the silence of our vulnerability. (*Word into Silence*, p. 49)

Christian faith has a special focus on the idea of salvation – a word that comes from *salus*, the name of the Roman goddess of personal health and social prosperity, related in the divine lineage to the Greek Hygieia ('Health') who was the daughter of Asclepius, the god of medicine and healing, and granddaughter of the great Apollo, the god of music, medicine, hunting and prophecy. Salvation, we can see, means more than being saved. It is about being well, getting better and flourishing.

> I have come so that you may have life, life in all its fullness. (Jn. 10:10)

Most of his contemporaries, it seems, saw Jesus primarily as a healer and a wonder-worker. There were other healers going the rounds of Palestine many of them healing for profit. Times have not changed that much if we look at TV evangelists. But Jesus performed his healings from compassion for the afflicted not for boosting his reputation. In fact, he frequently instructed those he had healed *not* to talk about it. Perhaps he felt it would distract people from the real message he was delivering. The healings illustrated something, but they didn't prove it. His physical healings do not need to be over-analysed. In a medical science that recognizes the placebo effect we are as open today to the immeasurable and mysterious in healing. There are healings that we would today call psychological and that Jesus linked to 'faith' which were actual signs of an ultimate wholeness and fullness which he called the Kingdom.

The healing influence of Jesus on those who turned to him in faith extended beyond the physical realm. After he healed the ten lepers or the woman with a haemorrhage, both socially excluding diseases, he addressed their re-integration with the wider community part of his therapy. He understood his mission as being to bring 'salus' – the health of salvation – to all. So he touched the sickness in us all for who is without need of healing?:

> If anyone hears my words and does not keep them, I do
> not judge him; for I did not come to judge the world but
> to save the world. (Jn. 12:47)

He is not, then, the saviour seen of the fundamentalist Christian condemning and damning those who do not take the medicine he offers. Later, Christian iconography portrayed him more in this style, as the Pantocrator, a universal judge with arm raised threateningly as in the Sistine Chapel. Later he was cast in the image of the divinised emperor ruling from his throne. But the earliest image of Jesus we have is that of a young shepherd, a Christian Apollo, carrying home the lost sheep on his shoulders. For the early church he was the 'all-healing word' as the Eucharist was the 'medicine of immortality.' Saviour: healer or judge? As we have seen with faith metaphors matter.

*

When the dominant metaphors about Jesus and Christianity reflect a religion with a weak contemplative dimension faith becomes fatally confused with belief. The ideas about Jesus, the theological formulas that define him, the rituals of worship, all become over-defined and defended, even absolutised and

idolized. No religion has put such value on doctrinal orthodoxy – uniformity of belief – as Christianity or been as antag-
onistic towards heresy. Of course all religions have their distinct
schools and traditions with degrees of in-house competition
and rivalry but Christianity, built on the founder's teaching
on non-violence, has often excelled in the brutality of its own
wars of religion. Enmeshed in European power-politics religious belief or affiliation often became a test of political loyalty
and heterodoxy a sign of treasonable tendencies. This fatally
blurred the distinction between faith and belief and even of the
inner and outer dimensions of religious experience. Despite a
strong mystical response to this process it led the institution
into a kind of sclerosis, a hardening of the arteries of faith and
contemplation, religious double-standard and spiritual shal-
lowness. If the most important thing is what you believe and
where you go to church, the equally important thing is what
you *say* you believe in order to stay safe. Religious belief and
external practice became increasingly a matter of social or legal
compulsion. What happens, in religion or communism, when
you are told what to believe – you believe nothing. So, go to
church, keep your head down and keep your doubts and questions to yourselves. No wonder that institutional Christianity
imploded so rapidly in its ancient heartland when modernity
dawned and freedom of personal choice, not social conformity,
became the higher standard.

I don't want to get side-tracked here by the woes of institutional Christianity today, but I think it is important to see
even very generally how we came to occupy what Charles
Taylor calls a 'secular age' and to understand the more subtle
meanings of secularism. The spiritual environment of our time
generally rejects organized structures of religion in favour of
personal experience. This can create much personal confusion
and the risks of an over-subjective new age mentality. Faith
and belief need to work together if spiritual development is to
unfold smoothly. Perhaps in the discovery that deep interiority

creates community, that meditation is a discipline not just a relaxation technique, that religions have a profound common ground as well as untranslatable differences we will find ways of building new religious forms from the ruins we presently inhabit.

When the contemplative dimension of the gospel is recognized and taught, the metaphors and forms of the church begin to change. They become more just and inclusive. Women find equality in a male-dominated world. Gays are not told they are 'disordered'. Sexuality is accepted and celibacy decriminalized. Issues of social and environmental justice become as important as protecting orthodoxy. When it breathes in the prayer of the spirit from the heart not just from public worship or private devotion the church experiences collectively the transcendence inherent in faith. Becoming less self-centred it sees that it serves but is not to be identified with the Kingdom it is meant to communicate. With the pure air of the contemplation faith grows and beliefs settle at the right level. The language we use about Jesus also changes. We no longer speak about him as if he were the captain of the winning team, defeating others, or as a judge come to condemn the world. The idea of sacrifice and redemption take on a more subtle and mystical meaning.

Understanding Jesus as the Divine Physician, the all-healing Word, the metaphors of a growing faith interact with the language of belief. The church begins to speak in a way the world can understand. This clarity between faith and belief marks the era of the early church when the great dogmas were being born from a dialogue between contemplation and reason, knowing and unknowing, mind and heart, scripture and prayer. Naturally, there was no period in history when the church was perfectly balanced. Institution and individual, contemplation and action, reason and revelation are innate tensions. It will never be easy to belong to the church. People stay in because it is harder outside. There conflict is inevitable and divisions to be expected but the great shapers of the Christian tradition moderated these forces by distinguishing between universal truths, faith and local practice. When Rome in the second century (already) excommunicated some local churches for following different dates of Easter, great souls like Ireneus of Lyons were shocked. Differences of practice, he said, do not compromise the unity of the faith. In fact he went further to affirm the value of diversity in a striking phrase that 'disagreement on fasting validates the agreement on faith'. Only a contemplative vision and a catholic mind can preserve unity in this generous and confident way.

The life of the early Christian communities is inspirational for us today and offers a necessary historical perspective on our present conflicts. To grow in faith in a Christian community needs a sense of tradition as well as a personal involvement with a contemporary community. The lineage and transmission that is really what the church is, flows from past to future through personal experience. We start from the gospels and are nourished by re-reading them. *Lectio*, reading with the heart and chewing the Word is a Christian practice that balances the spiritual diet. Whoever wants to grow in Christian faith needs, like the first Christians, to balance meditation and *lectio*, absorbing the Word and doing the work of silence.

The New Testament is best understood in its biblical and historical context but the scriptures as a whole are a unique form of sacred writing with unpredictable power to enlighten and open the mind and heart even for those who know very little of their context or history. Their form expresses their content – a story told from different perspectives, carrying a meaning that is not merely delivered but discovered. Interpretation is the heart of reading scripture. They are not *sutras*, philosophical statements or historical records. The gospel *is* the gospels: a four- dimensional narrative. The story produces its own commentary when read against the backdrop of our lives so that we become part of the story. In many of the gospel stories we are left wondering what happened next. How did Martha react to Jesus telling her to de-stress and meditate? What happened to the elder brother who was jealous of the treatment given the prodigal son? Did the rich young man who was too possessed by his possessions to follow Jesus ever get a second chance. *We* are what happens next – if we have read well.

Faith leads to love as we have already seen. Growing in faith is like continuing to fall in love, realizing that the relationship has a future and is not just a romance. When we meet someone and fall in love we feel that our two stories are mingling, distinct but united, and forming a new mysterious compound called relationship. Faith drives this process at every level on which we discover our capacity for love.

*

The Indian tradition distinguishes between primary scriptures and secondary commentaries, *srutis* and *smritis*. *Sruti* is what has been directly heard and *smriti* what is later remembered and reflected on. Distinguishing between direct experience and thought about experience should however not be made too much of an absolute. Direct experience can also be awakened by a reflective process because grace knows no boundaries. Nevertheless the distinction between thought and experience is helpful in developing the capacity for knowledge by unknowing and for understanding what we mean by Christian faith.

> may you know it though it is beyond knowledge. And so may you come to fullness of being, the fullness of God himself. (Eph. 3)

Christians accept this distinction too by going back repeatedly to the gospels as their primary source, always fresh, original, re-creative as the Word of God is, always 'alive and active' and cutting through the pride of thought that would otherwise block us from full knowledge. The commentaries on the

gospels layering through the centuries as the Christian tradition make us more receptive to the original text and send us
back to them with deeper curiosity and new insight. As direct
experience expands, so does our level of interpretation and
the silence that results form any true encounter in the spirit.
To deepen Christian faith this rhythm of word into silence, of
imageless and non-conceptual meditation and *lectio*, chewing
the inexhaustible Word, is necessary.

Without experiencing silence and scriptures in this way faith
in its Christian expression cannot mature. Yet meditation and
scripture are not the only means of growing faith in Christian
life. The one thing that holds all ways in harmony is love and
communion. Faith cannot grow without being active in love.
Even if we are not thinking of Christ we are meeting, serving and loving him in each other. So, there is also service of
others in whom we see Christ even if we don't recognize and
name him at the time. There is work, playing our social role
which is selfless as long as we are standing on the side of those
most in need. There is celebrating the Eucharist, the mystery of
the transforming delight of his self-giving presence. There are
innumerable other forms of worship, community-life and the
patient developing of our God-given gifts.

Often people who assume – or reject – Christian identity
know very little firsthand of these formative texts. They may
have heard them read out (inaudibly and without commentary)
in church or come across them in random quotes at funerals
and weddings. When they start to meditate many Christians
have little acquaintance of their scriptures. Yet the experience
they find in meditation sends them to search the scriptures to
find the meaning of what they are learning as well as to support the journey they have started. At the heart of the whole
experience, that embraces both the silence and the word, is the
person Jesus – not interpretations and commentaries on him,
not images and ideas but a presence, a love, in which I am also
present to myself in a wholly new way. Recognizing him is to

know what discipleship means and this is Christian faith. Faith is relationship, beliefs attempt to express it.

The gospels tell the story of Jesus of Nazareth, a preacher, healer, prophet, a social failure. The telling of the story of his life and death mysteriously merges into the experience of his presence. There are always new ways to tell the story. In Pasolini's black and white film version of the story, faithful to the words of the Gospel of Matthew the narrative is re-told in a new medium using non-actors, with just the words of the gospel and powerful images. We see a Jesus youthfully intense, passionate, single-minded, compassionate and fearless, but also filled with the mystery of the divine emptiness. However the story is retold, the more you get to know him the deeper he seems and the more his presence expands and pervades all reality in a way that transcends religion and the sacred. The gospel narrative tells us that it was this very depth and the demands it made that led many to stop following him.

This emptiness of infinite depth is what we mean by the mystery of Jesus. We begin to touch it in meditation. The divine emptiness can indeed be fearsome. But it also leads to a discovery of a new kind of connection in our human solitude, a falling in love that is not primarily emotional though it heals the emotions, a falling into self-knowledge in an intimacy that remains hidden and indescribable. It is not purely intellectual – it is not dependent upon a remembering of an historical figure – nor is it magic dependent on ritual or incantation. Christian faith does not give you a club key into a private room to which we have privileged access to chat with Jesus, get his take on things or have our needs instantly met. That would be a pastiche of faith, a virtual relationship similar to the intense but disembodied relationships of an internet chat room. The intimacy with Jesus that arises and develops in Christian faith is not an imaginary conversation revolving around my private desires and fantasies; it is not a mind game. Yet Christian faith develops a relationship with Jesus. This reflects a law we encounter in all relationships. Self-knowledge and love for the person with whom you are in relationship unfold synchronistically and together.

*

The Jesus known through a faith that grows within a Christian community (community means precisely that it is not a privatized or exclusive relationship) is more than an historical re-enactment. Faith doesn't conjure him up. There is an eerie room at Mount Vernon in Virginia which was George Washington's home and now more of a national shrine than a museum. In this room an actress, if that's the word, has studied and totally assumed the character of Mrs Washington. She sits knitting and chatting with the visitors and doesn't drop the persona for a second. In faith we don't have to go to such extremes of imaginative recreation, forming mental pictures of Jesus, having conversations with him. These are valid exercises of Christian prayer, similar to the visualization practised in some Buddhist disciplines, but they are preparatory, partial and open us to something much more real.

As John Cassian says in describing the difference between mental and spiritual vision:

> Every mind is upbuilt and formed in its prayer according to the degree of its purity. To the extent that it withdraws from the contemplation of earthly and material things its state of purity lets it progress and causes Jesus to be seen by the soul's inward gaze . . . For they will not be able to see Jesus coming in his royal power who cannot say with the Apostle: 'If we have known Christ according to the flesh, yet now we no longer do'. (Cassian, Conference X:vi)

'Pure prayer' in which all thoughts and images are laid aside was a cause of controversy even at the time of Cassian. In fact he sets the teaching on meditation in an account of the theological conflict that he called the 'anthropomorphic heresy'. He describes the anguish this caused a revered old monk of the desert called Abba Serapion who was clinging to the imaginative level of prayer. Eventually he was persuaded to let go of the images and slip into pure prayer. Doing this with a group of other monks one day he broke down in tears, fell to the ground and cried 'they have taken my God away from me and I do not know to whom I can pray'. It's a moving story of the challenge of shifting spiritual gears. But even more moving and reassuring is the support he received from the others with whom he prayed who comforted the old man and brought him back into their circle of faith-filled silence.

Even though meditation – pure prayer – became an integral part of the Christian spiritual tradition it remained personally challenging and institutionally controversial. At times of crisis the contemplative consciousness often awakens more powerfully. This happened in the dark days of the fourteenth century and it is at the heart of the renewal of Christianity in our own time when it is being practised on an unprecedented scale. The challenge does not only consist in the intrinsic difficulty of the practice. Poverty of spirit leading to purity of heart is not consolatory religion but religion-as-transformation which is inevitably difficult to sustain. The challenge for us today however is compounded by particular features of our time especially our exciting and uncomfortable pluralism. We are confronted more directly and on a larger scale than ever before with diverse expressions of faith and belief systems; through economic migration and globalization once isolated cultures and traditions are thrown against each other and cohabit. In the heartland of Western Christianity, the church is widely discredited. Formerly 'Christian societies' are now multi-faith. In France more Muslims go to mosques in France than Christians go to church. Modernity has created an inter-religious world but has yet to develop a language of faith that all can understand.

The Second Vatican Council anticipated this emergent diversity 50 years ago. In its prophetic spirit, the mind of the Council did not fear or condemn this development but unexpectedly affirmed a commitment to dialogue which has opened a new era in Christianity and all world religions. Teaching not just a pragmatic tolerance genuine respect and reverence, the Council declared that it 'rejects nothing that is true and holy in other religions' a monumental turn in consciousness, a seismic shift in the history of religion.

This is progress. Such a new approach for Christian faith towards other traditions is not less than an evolutionary leap in the understanding of what faith means. As a result it triggered a new understanding of spirituality because only this interior and depth dimension of religion can hold such an expansion of understanding. With this expanded perspective on the relationship of different expressions of faith a contemplative spirituality becomes necessary on a larger scale. What was once cloistered (at least so we imagined) in consecrated communities re-entered the mainstream. Now, when we ask what is the meaning of Christian faith, we do so within a framework of inter-faith understanding in which differences and similarities carry complementary weight. The age of intentional conversion has passed. The age of witness and dialogue has dawned. Dialogue has become an opportunity to develop Christian faith to a new maturity and universality but for many it is still hard to understand and a source of confusion or contradiction.

There are still Christians who think that dialogue itself breaks faith and makes us unfaithful to Christ because dialogue implies a level of equality and respect for the other's right to exist in its own way. To Christians of a fundamentalist orientation this betrays the Christ who declared 'no one comes to the Father except through me'. The new age of faith we have entered demands a new reading of the scriptures of our own faith tradition as well as knowledge of what others believe. There remain many today who reject this call and cling to an earlier form of Christianity. Yet record progress has been made in evolving Christian identity through the recovery of contemplative experience and through inter-religious dialogue. Those who face the challenge and take the risk of dialogue discover that they don't lose or betray faith but strengthen and deepen it.

*

On one of my first trips to Thailand I met and became friendly with an American Buddhist monk. He invited me to visit his monastery in the south of the country after my schedule of retreats to Christian meditators. When I arrived, I discovered my friend had been delayed for a couple of days. I felt a little stranded in a remote foreign place of a different religion and where I was also linguistically isolated. I accepted it as a day or two of being quiet and observing the life of the monks. I began to feel deeply but disturbingly impressed by the life and its atmosphere around me.

It seemed a genuinely contemplative monastery where meditation was central to its life. I knew enough to know that not all Buddhist monasteries in Thailand (or elsewhere) are like this. I was moved and impressed and felt my own original monastic impulse aroused in full vigour. I couldn't help but compare it with monasteries I knew in my own tradition where meditation was at best notionally acknowledged but not practised – and a few which would have been actually suspicious of it. I saw how universal and foundational meditation is as a wisdom way of faith and how sad it is not to see this is not universally recognized or practised by the very people the world should expect to look to for guidance and inspiration. Then I was suddenly and briefly taken offguard by a very disturbing thought. Why not stay here – where meditation was understood and practised, where it didn't need to be defended or justified to people who should know better? It wasn't a logical or thought-out idea but it was a strong emotional impulse. The grass looked much greener on this side, at least, for a short time. In the same moment I realized this would mean changing my way of faith, not a small issue to take account of. I can't say I seriously considered this or wanted to but it was disturbing to see that it could occur to me at all to follow a direction that would lead me to do this. I felt a flash of fear that I might be led to lose my faith or, as we might say in this context, that my faith might become more Buddhist than Christian. All this took only a moment to process but it was very disturbing to sense how my personal identity could be threatened. Might I prefer to stay where I found a commitment to a way of faith of a depth I had rarely found at home? Would I pay the price for this? Was my own identity so weak, my own faith-path so shallow to permit this to happen? I glimpsed the edge of the abyss we all walk beside each day without noticing.

The moment passed quickly. I didn't panic but waited for it to pass and now I would say my faith had been deepened through it. I also became grateful for that moment of uncertainty for another reason. It helped me to see how painfully anxious some Christians are when they are confronted by deep faith in other religions and why they can fear for their identity and why dialogue can seem like collaboration with the enemy. On occasions since when I have sat, feeling the hopelessness of talking about the broader dimensions of Christian faith with Christians of a very narrow or intolerant outlook, it has helped me feel some empathy with them by remembering this experience. I could sense the grip of fear that had entrapped them. It is an existential anxiety that involves not only the fear of becoming an apostate but also of losing one's core identity. It is in other words a fear of death. If you can't confront it you may well react violently and flee not only from dialogue but any human contact with the threatening other. On the other hand, if you sit it out and face down the fear you will find the identity that you so feared to lose re-clarified and reborn.

Inter-faith dialogue is a challenge and even a risk but it is also an opportunity to identify what Christian faith really means. Dialogue tests integrity because we have to face the honest question: Are we really interested in dialogue or are we secretly trying to convert the other person? Are we just going through religious motions with an unengaged heart? Are we being polite? Or are we really trying to see reality from the other's point of view? Over the years I have learned much about these unsettling questions from the Dalai Lama; how he really tries to see truth from the other point of view. He takes the risk and if he is frightened of doing so I haven't felt it. His Buddhist identity is unshakeable but inherently open and his faith is not undermined by his allowing full expression to his lively curiosity. This is not, I think, because Buddhism is 'non-dogmatic' and tests experientially whatever the practitioner is asked to take on trust only until experience proves it. Christians, by contrast, are depicted as being dominated by the need to believe the dogma, not to test it. In reality, Buddhists can be as dogmatic as anyone else at times and Christians can lay aside their thoughts and enter the silence which puts absolutely everything, dogma included, to the test.

The Christian enters this silence of God for the reason suggested in Simone Weil's saying that if we had to choose between Christ and the truth, we should choose the truth because we will not go very far before we fall into the arms of Christ who *is* the truth. This is a reminder to understand how dialogue deepens Christian faith. It tests our integrity and keeps us humble. In entering the silence of faith we see aspects of the truth from perspectives that we haven't seen yet from our safely familiar viewing points. Faith is a boundless panorama. It is continuously thrown more widely open as we re-adjust belief to the new intensity of faith that the changing view bestows. Similarly, after deep dialogue we return to our own scriptures and forms of worship with a new appreciation of how they relate to the way of faith.

This is one aspect of Christian faith today found in the encounter with other traditions. Another aspect is domestic, an internal family matter, the problem of the church.

*

Their problem with the church is frequently the reason people identify for drifting out of Christian faith, either into a no man's land of eclectic religious pluralism, a bit of this a bit of that according to what I feel like today, or seriously jumping the Christian ship into another tradition intending to go the rest of the journey that way. There are many problems with the church and always have been. Today these have received the full spotlight glare of publicity especially in the Catholic Church in the sexual abuse of children perpetrated by a few clergy and covered up by authorities more concerned for the church's reputation than for the past or possible next victims. There are other reasons why the church has lost credibility: the proud and tenacious clinging to institutional divisions, the emphasis on sexual morality over the demands of social just- ice and the environmental crisis and the reluctance to change forms to accommodate the norms of the modern era. Another reason is simply spiritual. People can tolerate a sinful and eccentric religious institution as long as it has not lost its spir- itual dimension. But when they feel the church is failing to provide the teaching and support for the long deep journey of faith they want to undertake they pull away.

Whether it is for social or spiritual reasons, many people today feel reluctant to admit publicly or even to their friends in other spheres of life that they are looking into the Christian path at all. I was once giving a retreat and a young woman came to see me. 'Oh, it's quite amazing,' she began, 'When I arrived Friday night, I noticed that a friend of mine from work was also here and she said, "Oh isn't it amazing that you're here too!"' I replied it was nice to discover you have something deeper in common with someone you just work with. But, she went on to say, my friend said to me 'but don't tell them that at work I was here, will you?' I imagine a Buddhist retreat would have been an ok way to spend a weekend but it was fashionably unacceptable to say 'I went to a Christian retreat last weekend'.

All Christians today are aware of their poor media image. They live with it in different ways, though of course some don't want to be associated at all with what seems like one of the big losers of our time.

The church (meaning all churches) is a great mystery not least of all because it survives its own self-destructiveness. Its management skills are often awful and its decisions often unjust; it can be hypocritical and not see it. It can persecute its own and give the cold shoulder to outsiders. Churches have much maturing to do regarding their attitudes to sex and much deepening with regard to prayer. Often it is dazzled by its own white magic. Even despite its virtues and its pockets of transcendent holiness it's amazing that it survives.

Maybe it is the 'deposit of faith' that saves it from itself. The church is somehow charged with the truth that Jesus spoke, the truth that Jesus is. In the continuous transmission of the Spirit it finds the resources for sharing this historically and geographically. And it carries an amazing, terrifyingly revolutionary message. It is not so surprising that any institution, carrying such a charge, often fails or even betrays its message and garbles it embarrassingly. It is easy to say, 'Would Jesus really have said that or put the emphasis there?' 'Is that Jesus speaking? Is that in the spirit of the gospels? Why complicate it all so much? Why create a bureaucracy to police belief when the gospel simply says to love one another?'

Like Jesus' first, and seemingly ill-chosen disciples, the church is 'slow to understand', slow and frail. The institutional church is the structure that generations of disciples have constructed and it has evolved according to sociological norms.

Even as a Catholic I can't understand how the hierarchy of the church is divinely constructed. Like all institutions it gathers momentum, is overweight and resists reform. All this makes it easier to forgive and live with.

The very weakness of the institutional church can however become a means of deepening faith. For one thing, they reveal some of the ways in which the church does actually succeed in its mission. Because I travel, I have had many opportunities to be impressed and proud of what the church does. In many places far from the centres of religious power, old nuns, young priests, middle-aged bishops, single women make heroic sacrifices within the church to serve the world. I have met parents who make the spiritual formation of their children a priority. Hard-working people run the spiritual and active works of their parish or local community. Business men and women struggle each day to synchronize their professional life with their faith and belief. People give to others when they are feeling the pinch themselves. In quiet and unacknowledged ways and supported by their life in the Christian community people serve as peacemakers of superhuman patience and integrity. All because their faith is lived and nourished in the church.

Ivan Illich saw that the deep structural flaws in the church resulted from its succumbing long ago to the temptation to acquire and hold on to power outside the spiritual realm. Very few can resist the offer of power. Jesus did in the desert when the devil took him to the top of the temple and offered him the kingdoms of the world. Few are not tempted to say, 'OK, I'll take this power conditionally because I'll make the world a better place.' In the same way we pray to win the lottery so we can fund good works with it.

Perhaps this is a double-bind the church has to live with. We all support what we don't agree with through our taxes, but paying tax is a condition of citizenship. Yet we can't forget that the desire for power over others is a relationship the gospel radically rejects. The clericalization of the church was one of the first ways it contradicted this. But how can you run a church without some kind of clergy? So it's not that the church shouldn't have clergy or religious orders; it needs them and some live their faith in these forms of life. But the clericalization of the Christian mind in a hierarchical, pyramidical structure became a symptom of succumbing to the temptation to power. Contemplative practice loosens up this spiritual sclerosis considerably. For clergy and laity alike and equally it opens a common ground where role-playing can be suspended and all can meet in the spirit. The weekly meditation group meeting in a parish is an example. One I know in Los Angeles is led by a woman parishioner but the parish priest attends faithfully, taking his seat alongside the other members.

Institutionally, the church can over-emphasize belief and structure and push faith to its margins. It can also persecute or wilfully ignore the prophets that God raises up within its ranks. The contemplative life revives this asphyxiation and keeps the oxygen of faith flowing so that we again see what is at the very heart of the church and what the church really means.

*

The crisis of the church is unfolding today in its deepest structures. A slow deconstruction of the old power system and a disengagement from traditional forms of being in the world is underway. It's a slow process as everything in the life of such a trans-historical, trans-cultural entity is likely to be and partly because the ecclesiastical attachment is so strong. So much is invested in it at the psychological and cultural level. Though its existing form can still be admirable and beautiful, something radically new is also appearing. As, from their different perspectives, both Karl Rahner and John Main saw the new Christianity will demand a deeper faith that will lead it more fully into its contemplative dimension and thus also radicalize its active expressions on. 'The Christian of the future will be a contemplative or there won't be any Christians', as Rahner, the best theologian of his era starkly prophesied.

When it breathes the oxygen of faith, the church speaks about Jesus and thinks less about itself. (How many sermons speak about Jesus, the mystery of who he is and the challenge of who we say he is?) It does not try to compete in the league tables of salvation with other religions. Its moral teaching becomes more balanced and realistic. But the church is composed of its members and faith is personal before it expresses itself socially. So the renewal of Christianity is incremental and begins at the grass roots before the leaders know what is happening.

In the middle of the process of change it is often hard to see the guiding hand of love at work. There is the feeling of loss, of uncertainty, of conflict and anger. But love, constantly evolving from eros through friendship to agape is the mystery unfolding. Christian faith is relationship to Jesus and like all relationships of love it has only one way to go, deeper, or to die. Meditation too is about relationship, with self, others and God and, as a work of pure attention, it is a work of love that changes us as it deepens us. As love shines on every part of us, even the darkest corners, we move into fullness of life.

The institutional church is like the battered cable that carries this energy of renewal. Sometimes it cracks and seems to interrupt the transmission of faith. But it is fixed by the very force it carries.

*

Instead of seeing only the flawed institutional structures faith allows us to perceive the mystical body of Christ. As faith grows so does the experience of the love that was stronger than death and that sent both him and ourselves back to the world to live here in a new way. Local, personal and global, Christian faith integrates and transcends individualism; it comes to maturity in community because salvation, the healing and restoration to wholeness, is interdependent.

In every faithful relationship we pass through stages and move onto different levels. Sometimes, moving into another stage, a beloved person can seem to become a total stranger. This awful loss may be lead to a new intimacy, a deeper union of friendship. Or it may not. There are no guarantees and the only certainty is change. Growth happens through crisis. Christian faith too, at the personal and collective level is in crisis. We go through stages in this relationship with Christ marked by new levels and stages of self-knowledge. And who is not in relationship with Christ as a universal teacher of humanity even if they reject the church that carries his name and message in the world? There are different kinds of relationship, different forms and degrees of faith. But if the person we are involved with is everywhere, then everyone has some kind of relationship with him.

As I described in my book *Jesus: The Teacher Within*, the first stage of faith is simple openness to Jesus as a reality in history. This may go no further and remain a largely conceptual matter. But if it leads to an awareness that this relationship is having a personal influence on the way we feel and live and that we are more whole as a result, then it has already moved to another level. This is a matter of pure awareness. The third level dawns with the sense of shifting boundaries and expanding horizons. Who on earth is he that we have begun to know and how do we feel that he knows us? Is he the one who is One, whom we have been waiting for, the Word made human?

What is the complete Christian? Who has ever had full Christian faith? Perhaps Jesus is the only real Christian because he has emptied himself into the Father who emptied himself into him. Jesus always points beyond himself to the Father. He is not an easy person to relate to for this reason, and to know him is to taste emptiness. Perhaps we are only Christian when we too are emptied – empty of desire and self-referencing – and find ourselves by the loss of self in a union with the one whose very presence is an invitation without coercion. What we can say, however, is that the growth of faith corresponds to the personal maturing of the individual. Only a very immature kind of faith needs to defend itself. As faith grows it turns us outwards with a new passion for inclusivity and unity.

Christian faith exists indestructibly but it is not unchanging. Irreducible to belief and free from the culture it creates, it is embodied not abstract. Having moved into a post-Christian world, after centuries of exporting and often imposing itself, the culture of Christendom is changing. The secular world in which Christian faith has now to grow has paradoxically been created by the Christian vision itself – the respect for universal human dignity, the significance given to marriage and ordinary life, the meaning of freedom. This suggests that faith is not bound to religious forms. A 'religionless Christianity' as imagined by Dietrich Bonhoeffer can at least be imagined. The social context in which faith grows is important but the essence of Christian faith is simply to find ourselves touched by the non-coercive power of Christ. The first conscious glimpse of that happening is knowing that we are being healed. Jesus once said to someone like us, 'your faith has healed you. Go on your way'.

> We prefer our self-protecting isolation to the risk of the face-to-face encounter with the Other in the silence of our vulnerability. We are reluctant to admit that we are the sick and sinful whom Jesus came to heal. (*Word into Silence*, p. 49)

8

Unity

The state of oneness is the goal. We approach it through degrees of unity. Understanding the meaning of unity accompanies faith at the personal level of growth in relationship to ourselves and to others. But it also manifests at the social and global levels as we endure the crisis of our time and the divisions and conflicts that it produces.

John Main understood meditation as a way of realizing the potential for unity that exists and waits to be realized in the depth of our nature:

> We have a principle of unity within our being and it is this, our spirit, which is the image of God within us.
> (John Main Talk)

Every act of faith that we make and repeat encourages the process of realizing this principle of unity in our way of life. Every faith act, like every meditation and every time we repeat the mantra, helps to integrate us a little more despite our inevitable failures and infidelities. We can always decide to come home again. We come back home to the same act of faith, to where we belong, just as we come back to the mantra whenever we get distracted. In significant relationships we come back to those people and commitments to which, in faith, we have given ourselves.

Understanding faith means seeing that every act of faith, whether successful or not, helps to make us more whole, more one. It integrates us through all the means that we have looked at so far, through waiting, through the purifying of spiritual vision, seeing things that the mind can't see; choice, prioritizing our lives, and therefore giving our lives order, centeredness, balance; and by transforming our experience of time. We become conscious of this integration through endurance, through patience and above all, through the self-transcendence by which every human person finds the space to grow.

*

The integrity that comes with faith has a moral dividend. The faithful person will become truthful, just, and peaceful because faith is the seed that opens up into love and all virtue is contained in love. *The beginning is faith; the end is love.*

Because of this unforced natural moral improvement we come to feel that meditation is *good* for us. We use the word 'good' to say many things but it means most by feeling the causal link between the daily practice and our being and acting better. The feel-good factor of meditation is not self-centred because it is hard won and changes everything from the way we think to the quality of our work. I once spoke to a conference of business school academics shortly after the collapse of Enron. They were reacting to the shocking news of corporate bad faith and to seeing some of their best former students led off in handcuffs. The academics were confused and questioning themselves. Should they have taught them differently? As educators what had they done wrong? They concluded the problem was that they had let the business ethics courses slip in favour of an obsessively more success and profit oriented training. I said I couldn't see this as the main cause for the wholesale collapse of a professional culture. Enron was only the biggest and worst of a more widespread corruption of standards. With or without ethics courses people know when they are lying and cheating. What was needed, it seemed to me, was that these driven, brilliant business minds allowed themselves enough space to experience their own essential goodness. Then the meaning of goodness in their personal and professional lives would become clear. When you know in your own experience that despite all your faults you are essentially good everything changes.

This experience of our essential goodness is simpler than and different from any other feeling. It belongs to a mystical level of integrity. The meaning of this wholeness is that same unity of the spirit that John Main speaks about, the 'principle of unity' that is within us by nature. It issues both from our own spirit, and, most wondrously, our likeness to God. It is at the same time the most obvious and most difficult thing to believe about ourselves

The twelfth-century monk Richard of St Victor said that the education of this mystical sense begins with self-simplification. That is, we grow spiritually and move into the contemplative dimension of faith by simplifying ourselves. As we become problems to ourselves, self-conflicted and contradictory or when we merely have too many things going on, too much stress, we thirst for this primal and ultimate simplicity. By the time we have lost it we may also have forgotten the name of what we have lost, what simplicity means and how to recover it. But even if it becomes a nameless desire, buried deep between layers of unreality, we long for it and this simplicity is the spiritual hunger of our era. When we hear about meditation we may feel this could possibly be what we are looking for. Only the simple can simplify us, though, and that is why it is so important to keep our approach to meditation simple – discipline rather than technique oriented.

Paradoxically we are reassured by discovering that that simple doesn't mean easy. In the ascetical, disciplined aspect of our daily meditation, the cleansing of memory, the clearing out of the old cupboards, the going into the locked rooms, facing submerged fears, we discover what simplicity really means. John Main makes no bones about this: he says we need determination and that more faith, not less, will be required as we progress. Approached in this way meditation is the best way to grow faith.

*

In time we see this verified externally both in personal relationships and in the work through which we relate to the world. Of course, our personal and global problems are highly complex and hard to grasp. It would be immensely naïve to say that meditation can solve them all immediately. However, just imagine, as John Lennon suggested. If the majority of humanity did meditate twice a day, if all schools taught meditation from primary level, if all political summits began with a period of meditation, if the markets meditated before trading, if physicians, therapists and patients built silence into their time together, might not the world be a saner and more civilized place? Violence –which degrades both victor and vanquished – would be reduced because the stress that leads to anger would be better controlled. It won't happen but it could and we can try to raise the level of spiritual consciousness through networks and communities that know this. One day we may glimpse how all humanity, with its irreducible diversity, is essentially a global parish. Even if the vision is a long time in the making we are the better for affirming it.

Meditation is personal, even solitary but it is not a privatized activity. Indeed it transforms us from isolated individuals into relational persons. Meditation therefore affects the world and its ways. The most recent financial crisis, one of a series that recurs by the decade, is widely accepted as having been caused by unregulated lust for short-term profit driven by ideas that bore no relation to real wealth. Abstract business thinking about derivatives and subprime mortgages produced complex financial instruments that even their perpetrators could neither fully understand or control. No God will solve this for us. Only the experience of God and our own goodness can solve the consequences of our fantasy and lack of common virtue. Pure prayer itself changes us because it makes us real and simplifies us. The financial breakdown of trust and probity was generated by a bankruptcy of the virtues we need for balance and health – moderation, prudence, justice. These virtues are, as the word itself means, *strengths* of the soul. We are designed in order to develop them. Meditation germinates the seeds of these inherent virtues and thus strengthens us to resist the false voices of their opposing vices.

Left to unravel unrestrainedly complexity ultimately explodes and like evil destroys itself and much else in its range of operation. Collateral damage after a financial crisis or a violent political revolution is like that of a natural disaster. It is extensive and takes many years to repair. We can't prevent a tsunami or an earthquake, but we can control ourselves. We need only to accept our limitations with faith in our potential to transcend them. The corrosive illusion is that we can buck mortality and ignore the limits of the material world. By keeping death 'constantly before our eyes', as St Benedict and the Buddha both recommend, meditation helps us to see the horizon and operate with a sense of perspective and proportion. The alternative is to be stuck in the cycle of illusion and disillusion. Opening Pandora's Box, as we do in imaginary economics, violent conflict or exploitation of the weak releases the demons of complexity and division that can today rapidly wreak disorder and suffering on a global scale. Nearly everything we do in these fields today is on a global scale. Our interdependence is therefore either a blessing or a curse.

Financially, socially, politically, ecologically, our crises illustrate a conflict of contradictory desires. We want many things and we can't have them all. Often they are so mutually contradictory that they can never be satisfied. A 2-year-old denied what it wants will rant and rage. So can an unenlightened consumer. The frustration that characterizes modern complexity feeds into the anti-social anger that possesses the urban psyche, especially among the young.

Escalating complexity lies at the root of our crisis. It clouds the vision of reality and creates endemic anxiety. Information technology produces tools that promise to relieve but often only exacerbate complexity and stress and we feel increasingly foreign to the wisdom that could save us. The first protest against this loss of wisdom was the Romantic movement in the eighteenth and nineteenth centuries. We have forgotten how the early Romantics were not escapists but political radicals and social activists. When Keats says 'Oh, for the life of sensation rather than of thought', he was protesting the cultural dislocation of sensibility that has reached critical levels today with our technical perfection of virtual reality. William Blake and D. H. Lawrence in their own ways struck out against the diminution of humanity caused by uncontrolled technical development.

Technology and science have brought many benefits. But at a high price. Many feel the cost is unsustainable and unjustifiable: the depersonalizing bureaucracies and erosion of civil rights, the commercialization of childhood, the commodification of sex, and the reduction of education to economic needs. Rage or depression are common and psychologically related reactions to these social developments. Prophets are meant to be angry when they confront untruth and injustice and Blake's outrage at the beginning of the industrial age at the ugliness of technology, and the over-rationalization of life still speaks to us. In this new world, as time lost its sacred dimension and became equated with money and everything became obsessed with economic performance, faith, that needs space to breathe and beauty to flourish, shrunk into belief. This became evident to poets and philosophers at the beginning of the industrial age two centuries ago. In the present digital age the stakes for survival are even higher.

We marvel at the handheld technology that reproduces reality for us or enables instant communication. We retreat into alternate computer worlds like *Second Life*, where people come home from work to go straight into a parallel virtual existence. For all its benefits technology can seduce us like idols of the past. It can render us incapable of wonder at the original of the things reproduced on our screens. The Upanishadic prayer for reality or the Psalms' description of idolatry have a poignant relevance in our age:

> Lead me from the unreal to the real; lead me from darkness to light. (Brihadaranyaka Upanishads)
>
> They have mouths, but cannot speak; eyes, but they cannot see (Ps. 135:16)

*

All prayer is directed to – and for – a heightened sense of reality. If it is made sincerely it is answered irresistibly. The essence of all prayer is attention and so it is through *pure prayer*, the simple work of attention, that we realize that what is granted in prayer – what we should be praying for – *is* the gift of prayer. Only then can we pass from the unreal to the real and be restored to first-sight.

Attention means more than the concentration skills needed for passing exams or learning the vocabulary for a new language. Learning to pay attention is the goal of all person-centred education. A capacity for sustained attention is necessary for compassion, for relationship and for restoring us to our core wholeness. The chronic distractedness and superficiality of much popular culture is a symptom of the crisis we have entered. Never has it been so obvious that it is the spiritual that directs the course of the material world. The shrinking attention span of modern consciousness seems to be connected to the high failure rate in long-term faithful relationships. The breakdown of fidelity – extended attention to the other in love – plunges many individuals and families into catastrophe which is a far worse state than crisis. Crisis, properly accepted, leads to growth. Catastrophe wrecks lives and can lead to meltdown.

Teaching children to meditate is not only good for them laying a vital discipline for their future lives. It is also good for us because in teaching children to meditate we re-learn what attention means. We learn that meditation is simple and natural and that it is not competitive. So, even though we may never be perfect meditators, we can do it by drawing upon the natural capacity and attraction to meditation that is so evident in children and remains inherent in the adult however overlaid by distraction and anxiety. It takes us time to perceive the fruits of the practice but in children it is apparent from the outset.

Attention purifies; faith unifies. The recovery of balance, prudence, wisdom, justice and inner strength, the traditional 'cardinal virtues', is the moral priority for a world increasingly globalized but dangerously divided. This has become so increasingly obvious after the recent financial shambles that what is called 'spirituality' is no longer embarrassing to the leaders of social institutions – medicine, education and business. The return of the spiritual in a culture so oriented to instrumentality – using, exploiting and discarding – brings the danger that spiritual practice comes to be seen as a technique of relaxation or self-therapy. Meditation needs to be practised. It first needs to be well taught.

Perhaps we are indeed awkwardly beginning a new era of human culture, conscious of our unity and open again after a long sleep to the meaning of faith. Perhaps we are again recovering the gift and wonder of first sight, knowing things with the wisdom of a child seeing the world with new eyes. Even when it is only weakly understood the spiritual dimension of transcendence and compassion is being awakened in the institutions of a culture that has become so obsessed with profit at any cost. It's a beginning. Globalization, it seems, is an irreversible force in the world economy but though it might prepare for a higher level of unity it does not mean unity. In fact, without a spiritual awakening to match an interior expansion to the external growth of human activity, a global economy may cause global conflict on a scale hitherto unimagined.

The need to recover what John Main called a 'principle of unity within us' could be met through a simple, daily practice of stillness and attention. That principle is universal and indicates that every person, regardless of their economic value or cultural standard, is an icon of the divine. The poorest farmer in India or Africa or a celebrated academic, an international statesman or financier living in a gated community with his privileged family or a migrant domestic worker separated from her family for years in a foreign land, can meditate and can meditate together because every human being is equally an actual icon of the divine. What the 12-step group shows about the democracy of the therapeutic recovery process the meditation group can show about the unity of the human spiritual family.

It is easier today to see the relationship between meditation and work – especially honourable, good and meaningful work. As the nature of work changes in the wake of techno-science the question of what is good work presses upon us all. For many, the dignity of earning their own living is denied. 'Happy is the person who finds their work,' the Upanishad tells us. 'Happier still is the one who knows that silence is work', it continues. The inner work of faith that is the discipline of meditation influences our concept of daily labour and reward. Life and work that lack this interior sense of meaning collapse into the narrow confines of the individual ego. Balance, wisdom and integration are lost. We work ourselves to death or, if we are denied work, we drive ourselves to death by distraction. Inner or outer, work is not just about self-fulfilment or say it fulfils us because it is about self-giving. It is done through community, tested through solitude, refined through mistakes as well as through breakthroughs. The fruit of good work is personal integration and unity with others.

*

'Where the spirit is, there is unity,' says St. Paul. This is a universal wisdom expressed in all the religious traditions. From the *Upanishads* again with its sense of the gathering together of all in the spirit:

> Radiant in his light, yet invisible in the secret place of the heart; the spirit is the supreme abode where dwells all that moves and breathes and sees. Know him as all that is and all that is not, the end of love longing, beyond understanding, the highest in all beings.

It's this insight into the unity at the heart of reality that meditation practises. At the core of all religion a way of faith is taught that is the way of silence, stillness and simplicity. Lived out as a daily practice it balances the conscious, rational, planning, judging, instrumental mind with what is deeper than thought or imagination. Our neolithic ancestors gathered at sunrise and sunset each day in their stones circles or by their standing stones. We have forgotten what they believed but those sacred places remind us of their faith and how they welcomed the miraculous birth of each day and were blessed by the sad beauty of its dying.

When we say we are too busy to meditate morning and evening are we more evolved, more conscious, more civilized than they were? Civilization rests on faith not technology. Faith leads to the belief in human goodness and equality, to trust in our neighbour, a sense of the common good rather than just selfish advantage, a passion for justice and a courage for compassion extended to the vulnerable. It empowers forgiveness and patience in times of betrayal and conflict.

Civilization also rests upon sustained faith in the future, believing that there is a point to it all, that we have not achieved perfection but we're not going to give up. 'We don't have to succeed, but God does not permit us to give up.' Civilized society rests on the belief born of faith that we have something worthwhile to leave for the next generation to perfect better than we were able to.

Meditation begins and ends in faith. It expresses the unity of all in the spirit, as do indeed all sacred acts inspired by love or compassion. Meditation as we can testify creates community experienced in the deep silence of being together. What silence makes happen is the transformation of consciousness and the emergence of a catholic mind, because catholic knows no boundaries and seeks to integrate all.

The modern world in crisis needs this catholic mind that exists in our deep nature, the universal consciousness. It is seeing with new eyes the primal and ultimate unity of humanity and our unity with the cosmos. The meaning of wholeness can not be measured against anything less than this unity.

Every expression of faith points this way. This is how the Christian sees it:

> until we all attain to the unity inherent in our faith and our knowledge of the Son of God, to mature humanity measured by nothing less than the full stature of Christ. (Eph. 4:13)

In a spirit of love we fully grow up into what Christ is. The new self which is formed as we grow in faith is pervaded by Christ, the new Adam, who recapitulates, assumes all matter and raises it to the incandescence of spirit. Then what we know as divided is united; what we suffered as discord becomes peace.

*

At the end, if any end exists, unity flowers in silence, the kind of silence we taste in meditation. Unity is self-repairing, boundless; there is no limit to it. As unity becomes more conscious we learn to live better with the contradictions, conflicts and sufferings of the dualistic world made by the dualistic mind. We see this world in the experience of non-duality and its brokenness becomes an opportunity of grace to serve others, to heal, to love.

UNITY

Every spiritual tradition is poised in the cusp of this unity. Explicitly in Jesus we see the paradox of death and resurrection that lies at the heart of the mystery; we pass through this paradox in order to enter into the saving knowledge. Human consciousness springs from this wisdom and we cannot escape from the human family or its law, just as we can't escape from the blood family and culture that we are born into. Unity is our common destiny but we die to ourselves as individuals in order to achieve it.

Jesus experienced this unity with the 'Father' even before his death and it seems to have pervaded all he felt, thought, spoke and did. Yet he had to die and pass through the state of separation and the experience of total loss. Even he had to feel abandoned by the Father and be plunged into *kenosis*, the ultimate emptiness before he could come to the fullness of union. This is the human paradox we all have to undergo personally. It's not headline-catching stuff. It can't be sold on the basis of the instant benefits it brings. It's not easily turned into a programme or a commodity you can sell. Yet we live into this mystery each day through faith. The Christian becomes conscious of sharing in what Julian of Norwich calls the spiritual thirst of Christ. It is the love longing that will always be until the one-ing of humanity happens. His thirst and love-longing, she says, is to have us all together, whole in him in his joy. The spiritual thirst lasts in him as long as we are in need and it draws us up into his bliss. The meaning of faith is the inextinguishable and insatiable longing of the human heart for union with that power of love, both creative and healing, that it finds is being poured into itself – a power with which it falls in love over and over again but will never fully understand and that, each time, it sees for the first time.

Afterword

Faith is more than belief. But to have faith is to believe in the journey of life seen *as* a way of faith. This just means that all faith in one sense begins with an act of faith in oneself. This is why I have kept referring to meditation because, to sit in meditation does not require any system of belief as such, but to persevere with it certainly demands faith in oneself. That's how the journey begins and keeps on re-inventing itself. As faith is above all about relationship, commitment and transcendence, so that a faithful life begins with self-acceptance and grows by discovering our capacity to leave self behind.

Community – like marriage and other civilized institutions, it is an outcome of faith – is the context in which we develop. As we become part of the community, what happens to the community happens to us, and what happens to us is felt through the community. The best metaphor for this, as St Paul realized, is the body itself.

So, after 20 years of seeing our meditation community grow in ways I never expected, I began to wonder where we were heading. The simplicity of the teaching remained the root value but it had generated many branches that were shaking hands with the branches of neighbouring trees. The future is always with us even when we try to live in the present moment. People were asking more regularly, 'what will happen when Laurence's plane goes down one day?' Even apart from succession planning, it was clear that some community structures needed updating to accommodate the new growth.

For quite a period of time I had no answer to this phase of our journey. On Bere Island, my hermitage base, I walked the cliffs, looked for revealing patterns in the sea stretching out towards an ever shifting horizon and pondered the options.

I wondered whether I should just stay put there, although the time didn't seem quite right for that. Then the need to move our young meditators' community to a new location in London proved the catalyst to developing what was the right thing for this moment – the vision of '*Meditatio*' the outreach program of The World Community for Christian Meditation.

The Meditatio Seminars are allowing for broad dialogue in which our branches may drop some fruit into the secular fields of education, mental health, leadership, business and the environmental crisis. Meditatio's work in developing spiritual networks for young people and a base of personal formation for some of them is also part of the *Meditatio* vision. And our technology of communication and web presence has become fun and fruitful.

Meditatio, then, is like another beginning and perhaps faith is a journey of endless beginnings. Faith grows and takes us forward by surprises, around bends we once thought were dead ends. Often, too, what is happening now seems to summon up earlier phases of the journey. Sometimes it feels as if we have to repeat what was not fully realized in the past or correct forgotten mistakes. We do get second chances, even if the best of them are only seen as such in retrospect. Yet very strangely too, as I recognize in active memory the resonances, echoes and parallels of what we are doing now with how we started, I wonder whether beginning and end are the right terms to describe the way of faith; whether something in between the two isn't in fact simply the unfolding of something unbelievably obvious and present.

Starting to Meditate

What is meditation?

Meditation is a universal spiritual wisdom that leads in silence, stillness and simplicity from the mind to the heart. It has many expressions and names. In the Christian tradition it is also called prayer of the heart or contemplative prayer.

The practical way of meditation taught by John Main is the faithful repetition of a prayer phrase or 'mantra' as he called it. He refound this way of prayer in the teachings of the early Christians, the desert fathers and mothers. In the fourth century they retired mainly to the desert of Egypt to live an authentic Christian life based directly on the gospel teaching of Jesus.

The phrase John Main recommended is 'Maranatha'. He chose this word because it is the oldest Christian prayer in Aramaic, the language Jesus spoke. Moreover, the word has no associations for us, so it won't give fuel to our mind eager to go on thinking. The faithful and loving repetition of this prayer leads us to stillness of body and mind and helps us to enter the silence that dwells in the centre of our being. The famous fourteenth-century mystic Meister Eckhart said: 'Nothing is so much like God as silence.' In Christian faith there in the silence of the true centre of our being dwells Christ, and there we enter the prayer of Jesus. John Main said in his last writing 'Moment of Christ':

It is our conviction that the central message of the New Testament is that there is really only one prayer and that this prayer is the prayer of Christ. It is a prayer that continues in our hearts day and night. I can describe it only as the stream of love that flows constantly between Jesus and his Father. This stream of love is the Holy Spirit.

Our first aim is to be able to keep our mind on the mantra during the meditation period. This is quite difficult in itself, as thoughts keep coming in. Our mind just loves going off on flights of fancies, down memory lane, or listing all the tasks we have to do after meditation. We just need to be patient and gentle with ourselves. When you realize you have got lost in your thoughts, don't judge or criticize yourself, but gently steer your mind back to your prayer word. Just accept that this is natural and to be expected. Your mind is like a playful puppy, always willing to run off rather than stay near you. You would not get cross with a puppy, would you? You would gently and lovingly encourage it to come back.

As long as you do this without any sense of forcing yourself – don't use the mantra as a club to hit your thoughts with – slowly you will be able to say the mantra without being aware of distractions. Your thoughts may still be there in the background, but more like music in the supermarket – you don't notice them very much. The more you practice the easier it gets and soon instead of saying the word, you seem to be listening to it and finally it will sound by itself in your heart. Then your body and your mind become like the centre of your being in harmony and at peace.

In *Word into Silence* John Main describes this as follows:

The surface areas of the mind are now in tune with the deep peacefulness at the core of our being. The same harmonic sounds throughout our being. In this state we have passed beyond thought, beyond imagination, and beyond all images. We simply rest with the Reality, the realized presence of God Himself dwelling within our hearts. (*Word into Silence*, p. 15)

The universality of meditation

Meditation is a universal spiritual discipline central to most of the world religions and wisdom traditions. There are many different forms of meditation in these various traditions, all equally valid in their own way. In all of them the emphasis is on practise and experience rather than theory and knowledge.

It is also an authenticated and ancient discipline in Christianity, although it sometimes seems as if that this is Christianity's best-kept secret. Jesus taught contemplation and that is the reason why this way of prayer flourished especially in the fourth century among the desert fathers and mothers of Egypt and Palestine, who based their life on Jesus' example. John Cassian collected their teachings in his book *Conferences*. It is in these writings that John Main rediscovered the tradition and opened it up for all people, calling it Christian Meditation. It is not only the way of prayer of the desert fathers and mothers but also of countless Christian mystics throughout the ages up to our present time. It is also a way of prayer established long before the Reformation and before the split between Roman Catholicism and Eastern Orthodox Christianity. It is therefore a beautiful ecumenical way of praying together.

All ways of prayer are valid but meditation is the missing dimension of much Christian life today. It does not exclude other types of prayer and indeed deepens reverence for the sacraments and scripture. The connection between all forms of prayer can be caught through the image of an old-fashioned wooden wheel:

The purpose of a wheel is to move a cart. Prayer is the wheel that moves our life spiritually towards God. To turn, the wheel must make contact with the ground. If the wheel does not touch the ground, it cannot move the cart; the wheel will just spin. So there must be a real time and place in our daily life that we give to prayer. The spokes of the wheel are like the different forms of prayer. All forms of prayer are valid and effective.

We have the Eucharist, intercessory prayer, the sacraments, the reading of Scripture and personal devotions. What holds the spokes together and turns the wheel is the hub. The spokes converge at the hub. We can think of the hub as the Prayer of Christ dwelling in our hearts. At the hub of the wheel, there is stillness. Without the still point at the centre, the wheel cannot turn.

Meditation is coming to stillness at the centre of our being. When we meditate, we come into that central stillness which is the source of all our action, our movement towards God through Christ within us. The movement of the wheel requires stillness at the centre. This is the relationship between action and contemplation.

How did John Main learn about meditation?

John Main was introduced to meditation through the universal tradition when he was serving in the British Colonial Service in Malaya. During the course of his duties there he met Swami Satyananda, founder of the 'Pure Life Society', who lived a life of immense generosity and depth dedicated to serving others. John Main was impressed by the serenity and the holiness of this monk and when the official business was over they started talking about prayer, especially about the Swami's way of repeating a mantra during the whole period of his meditation. Soon John Main found himself asking the Swami whether he as a Christian could learn to pray in this way. The Swami told him laughingly that it could only make him a better Christian!

In *Christian Meditation – The Gethsemani Talks* John Main recounts how the Swami stressed the importance of meditating each morning and each evening for half an hour, saying:

If you are serious and if you want to root this mantra in your heart then this is the minimum undertaking . . . During the time of your meditation there must be in your mind no thoughts, no words, no imaginations. The sole sound will be the sound of your mantra, your word. It is like a harmonic. And as we sound this harmonic within ourselves we begin to build up a resonance. That resonance then leads us forward to our own wholeness . . . We begin to experience the deep unity we all possess in our own being. And then the harmonics begins to build up a resonance between you and all creatures and all creation and a unity between you and your Creator.

This was the start of John Main's journey of meditation. Meditation leads into the silence conducive to contemplative prayer, deep silent prayer, and it became the mainstay of his prayer life and his whole existence, and finally led him to become a monk. At that time meditation was not accepted as a valid Christian way of prayer and he had to relinquish it on becoming a novice, which he did in the spirit of Benedictine obedience. He sorely missed it though, but saw it as being taught a form of detachment: *I learned to become detached from the practice that was most sacred to me to me and on which I was seeking to build my life. Instead I learned to build my life on God himself.*

Many years later he re-discovered the practice that he had been taught by the swami in the writing of John Cassian, a Christian monk, a desert father of the fourth century CE. There as he later wrote in the talks he gave on meditation at Thomas Merton's monastery, Gethsemane Abbey, he read of *the practice of using a single short phrase to achieve the stillness necessary for prayer.* I felt I had *arrived home once more and returned to the practice of the mantra.*

Why meditate?

The impetus for starting to meditate can often be a moment when we are faced with something out of the ordinary.

Something shakes us out of our ordinary perception of reality. It can be a crisis point or major life event at any stage in our lives, when the seemingly secure and unchanging reality we live in is bewilderingly turned upside down: we are rejected by an individual or a group; we face failure, loss of esteem; we lose a treasured job or our health suddenly fails us. The result can be either a refusal to accept the change, a descent into negativity, mistrust and despair. Or faced with the fact that our reality is not as immutable as we considered it to be, we may rise to the challenge to look at ourselves, our habitual framework, our opinions and values with different eyes.

Sometimes it can be a moment of exquisite beauty that makes us realise there is more than meets the eye. Bede Griffiths describes how awareness of true Reality did not spring out of a crisis but out of contemplation of Nature. He describes in *The Golden String*' how he was led by the beauty of bird song and hawthorn bushes in full bloom to a profound feeling of awe at the sight of the setting sun, while a lark *'poured out its song'.* He felt that he *'was made aware of another world of beauty and mystery'* and especially at evening he felt on many other occasions as well the *'presence of an unfathomable mystery.'*

It is not always so dramatic a moment; perceptual awareness varies from person to person, from moment to moment. Some of us may have had a moment of *'transcendence'*, an awareness of a different reality, an escape from the prison of the *'ego'*, whilst listening to music, poetry or being absorbed in a work of art. Others may never have been consciously aware of an actual moment of insight, and yet at some level may always have been aware of the existence of a higher reality and are without knowing becoming gradually more in tune with this reality. Quite early on in meditation we often touch the experience of real peace and even joy bubbling up. Moments like these when we are released from self-preoccupation are divine gifts.

In any case, this glimpse is not the end, but the beginning: an impetus for growth. The longing to know more about this intuited reality gets stronger and we look round for those who could help us to approach it. At this point we often discover meditation in one form or another. It is the start of the work of clarifying and integrating the experience and so allowing the ascent to spiritual awareness, personal authenticity and a transpersonal Truth.

The fact that an insight, a glimpse of another reality, is often the start of our journey into deeper prayer also means that we cannot bring anyone to meditation, who has not felt this longing need for 'more' in their own being. When meditators feel called to start a group, all we can do is advertise it and invite people. Whether those who turn up start meditation as a discipline of prayer is not our responsibility. We can't 'convert' others to meditation. But we can welcome, explain and encourage them to try.

How do we prepare for meditation?

John Cassian had sat at the feet of the Christian hermits in the desert of Egypt to learn about prayer in an authentic Christian life. Cassian stressed that this practice led to the silence of 'pure' prayer, contemplative prayer, without words and images. *'The mind thus casts out and represses the rich and ample matter of all thoughts and restricts itself to the poverty of a single verse.'* He continued by stressing the importance of the mantra: *'This mantra must always be in your heart. When you go to sleep let it be by saying this verse, till having been moulded by it you grow accustomed to repeat it even in your sleep.'*

The faithful repetition of a prayer phrase, just saying our word is, however, not as easy as it sounds. We need to prepare for this period; we can't expect to become fully focused on our prayer without preparation. When John Main was asked, how we should prepare for meditation, he said *'by many kind acts'*.

We have to be in the right frame of mind; trying to meditate after a heated argument with someone is not really going to work, is it? Our ordinary life and our prayer life are not separate: 'As you live, so you pray' was a very common saying amongst the early Christians.

In the world, in which we live, our lives tend to be busy and stressful. If we find that we are really very tired, it may well be advisable to have a short nap before we come to our yoga exercises. Doing a few yoga stretching exercises, a Tai Chi movement or two will also help to get the energy flowing. Otherwise all we will be doing is 'holy dozing', and that is alright too, but often it is accompanied by the sweet sound of snoring! Snoring and other noises that occur during meditation, however, can actually be excellent practice in detaching ourselves from extraneous matters and gently coming back and focusing on our word. Noises on the whole do not really disturb us, as long as we do not get irritated by them. We just need to accept that that is the way it is. No judging, no criticizing.

The reason we sit with our backs straight and our shoulders back and relaxed, is that this position also helps us to stay awake: our chest is free and open, so that we can breathe well and oxygen can flow freely round our body keeping us alert. Relaxing and falling asleep – however much needed – is of course not the purpose of meditation; the focused attention needed for meditation is in fact a way to alertness and being energized. It may help to start our session with a few deep breaths into the abdomen, which both relax and energize us.

The essential task in meditation is 'to say your word'. That is the focus. The word John Main recommended is 'maranatha'. It is the oldest Christian prayer in Aramaic the language Jesus spoke. We say it as four equally stressed syllables - ma-ra-na-tha. It does not matter, whether you say it with an English 'th' or with a 't' sound . The pronunciation is not that important. What is important is that you say it with full attention, lovingly and faithfully. Whenever your thoughts have distracted you, just gently bring your mind back to the word. Some people find it helps them to let the word rest on the breath, but if that causes distractions just focus on your word and say it at the speed and in the way that best suits you.

Sit down, sit still, with your back straight. Close your eyes lightly and begin to say your mantra. Stay with the same word throughout the meditation and from day to day. Let it take root in your heart and it will open up the grace of continuous prayer during the day and the night. Let go of all thoughts (good and bad ones alike). Meditate twice a day, early morning and early evening are the best times. If you feel you want to but don't have the time, learn from someone who is busier than you and who does make the time each day. Don't evaluate or analyse your meditation too much. Allow it to become, both interiorly and externally, a way of faith.

The World Community for Christian Meditation and Meditatio
www.wccm.org

The Community took form in 1991 inspired by the vision of John Main. It continues his work of teaching Christian Meditation and the work of restoring the contemplative as an essential and central dimension of all Christian spirituality.

John Main, a Benedictine monk, recovered a simple meditation practice in the contemplative tradition of Christianity and, most significantly, made it available to everyone. He started this work in 1975 when he founded the first Christian Meditation Centre in London. When he died in 1982, he was succeeded by Laurence Freeman, a Benedictine monk who is now the Director of The World Community for Christian Meditation. The World Community is an ecumenical, contemplative community with a strong commitment to inter-religious dialogue and emphasizing the link between contemplation and action.

The World Community for Christian Meditation has a presence in over 100 countries. Over 2000 groups meet weekly in homes, churches, community centers, hospitals, hospices, schools, prisons, universities and places of work – these groups, made up of people from all walks of life, committed to a daily practice of meditation, are the foundation of the community. It has its International Centre, the London Christian Meditation Centre and Meditatio Centre in London; the John Main Centre for Meditation and Inter-Religious Dialogue in Georgetown University, USA together with many other centres that serve the work of the Community around the world. The Community is thus a 'monastery without walls', a global family of emerging and national communities.

Being ecumenical, the community serves a universal 'catholic' unity in its dialogue both with Christian churches and other faiths. It nurtures inter-religious dialogue and has met particularly with Buddhists and Muslims in recent years. It encourages and supports the daily practice of meditation knowing its power to change hearts and so to transform the world.

Three of the major international events which are held annually are the John Main Seminar, The Way of Peace and the Silent Retreat at Monte Oliveto Maggiore, Italy. There is a rich and diverse program of retreats, talks, seminars, workshops, groups in all the countries reflecting local needs and interests. An important new development is the teaching of meditation to children which was pioneered in the Catholic Diocese of Townsville in Australia. Medio Media is the communication and publishing arm and offers a wide range of books, cd's, DVDs and videos to support the practice of meditation. Some of these have been translated into17 languages

Meditatio is a new outreach for the Community in the sharing and extension of the fruits of meditation in our community with the wider world. Launched in 2010 with a 3-year program Meditatio includes a series of contemporary seminars and workshops on focused themes ranging from Education, Business and Finance, Mental Health, the Environment to Inter-Religious Friendship and Collaboration and Citizenship. The life of an inclusive Christian contemplative community thus brings the fruits of the spirit into touch with the problems and crises of our time.

WCCM Centres and Contacts Worldwide
www.wccm.org

If you would like to receive more information about the Community, its work and publications, please contact:

INTERNATIONAL CENTRE

The World Community for Christian Meditation
St Mark's, Myddelton Square
London EC1R 1XX, UK
Tel +44 20 7278 2070
Fax +44 20 7713 6346
welcome@wccm.org
www.wccm.org

For countries not listed below, contact the
International Centre or visit www.wccm.org

Argentina	meditacioncristianagrupos.blogspot.com
Australia	www.christianmeditationaustralia.org
Belgium	www.christmed.be
Brazil	www.wccm.com.br
Canada English	www.meditatio.ca
Canada French	www.meditationchretienne.ca
China	www.wccm.hk
France	www.meditationchretienne.org
Germany	www.wccm.de
Hong Kong	www.wccm.hk
India	www.wccm-india.org
Indonesia	www.meditasikristiani.com
Ireland	www.christianmeditation.ie
Italy	www.meditazionecristiana.org
Malaysia	wccm.malaysia@gmail.com
Mexico	www.meditacioncristiana.com
Netherlands	www.wccm.nl

New Zealand	www.christiameditationnz.org.nz
Poland	www.wccm.pl
Portugal	www.meditacaocrista.com
Singapore	www.wccmsingapore.org
South Africa	www.wccm.co.za
Spain	www.meditaciocristiana.cat
Switzerland	deborah.walton@gmail.com
Thailand	bkkemilie@gmail.com
United Kingdom	www.christian-meditation.org.uk
United States	www.wccm-usa.org
Venezuela	www.meditadores.blogspot.com

Suggested Reading

Many resources for starting and continuing with meditation are available on the WCCM website:
www.wccm.org

Meditation

Laurence Freeman, *The Selfless Self*, Canterbury Press, Norwich, 2009

John Main, *Monastery Without Walls*, Canterbury Press, Norwich, 2006

— *Moment of Christ*, Canterbury Press, Norwich, 2009

— *Word into Silence*, Canterbury Press, Norwich, 2009

— *Silence and Stillness in Every Season: Daily Readings*, Medio Media, Singapore, 2010

Kim Nataraja, *Dancing With Your Shadow*, Medio Media, Singapore, 2006

— *Light Within*, Canterbury Press, Norwich, 2010

Peter Ng ed., *The Hunger for Depth and Meaning*, Medio Media, Singapore, 2008

— *Jesus: The Teacher Within*, Canterbury Press, Norwich, 2011

The Desert Tradition

John Cassian, Conferences, ed. B. Ramsey, Newman Press, New Jersey, 1997

Benedicta Ward, ed, *The Desert Fathers: Sayings of the Early Christian Monks*, Penguin Classics, London, 2003

Rowan Williams, *Silence and Honey Cakes*, Lion Hudson, Oxford, 2004

Inter-Religious Dialogue

The Dalai Lama, *The Good Heart: The Dalai Lama Explores the Heart of Christianity and of Humanity*, Wisdom Publications, Boston, 2005

Laurence Freeman, *Common Ground*, Continuum, New York, 2000

Religion and Society

David Cayley, *The Rivers North of the Future: The Testament of Ivan Illich*, Anansi, Toronto , 2005

Richard Rohr, *A Lever and a Place to Stand*, Paulist Press, New York, 2011

Charles Taylor, *Sources of the Self: The Making of the Modern Identity*, Cambridge University Press, Cambridge, 1989

— *A Secular Age*, Harvard University Press, Cambridge, 2007

Simone Weil, *Waiting for God*, Harper, New York, 2009